INDIAN

COSTUMES

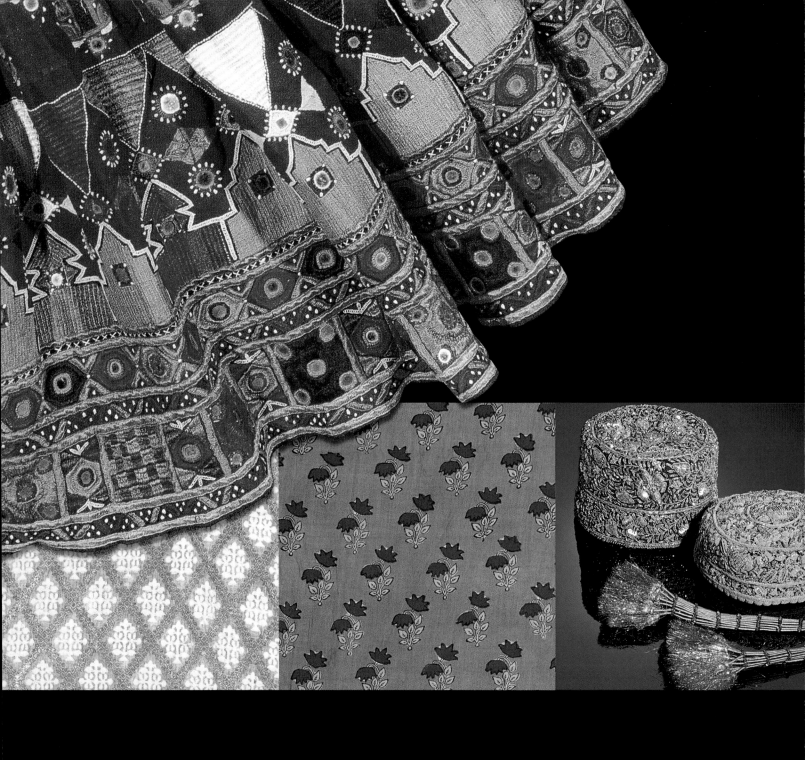

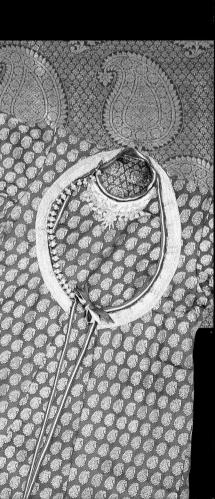

INDIAN
COSTUMES

A N A M I K A
P A T H A K

Lustre Press
Roli Books

ISBN: 81-7436-376-9

© This edition Roli & Janssen BV 2006
Published in India by
Roli Books in arrangement with
Roli & Janssen BV, The Netherlands
M-75, Greater Kailash II Market, New Delhi 110 048, India
Ph: ++91-11-29212782, 29210886; Fax: ++91-11-29217185
E-mail: roli@vsnl.com; Website: rolibooks.com

Text: © Anamika Pathak
Editors: Dipa Chaudhuri / Padma Pegu
Design: Arati Subramanyam
Layout: Naresh Mondal
Production: Naresh Nigam

Printed and bound in Singapore

CONTENTS

A BRIEF HISTORY OF INDIAN COSTUMES

Across the world the sari and blouse are invariably evocative of the Indian woman's typical attire, and the *dhoti* and *kurta,* of the Indian man's attire. In India unstitched garments are as popular as stitched ones. Local variations are identifiable in traditional costumes used by men and women. The most popular garments used by Indian men, however, are the *kurta,* the *paijama* or the *dhoti,* and the turban; the long shirt or *phiran;* the *salwar;* and the *achkan* or *sherwani,* the *paijama,* and the turban. Similarly, the typical Indian women's garments are the *kurta, salwar* and *odhani;* the *ghagra, choli* and *odhani;* and the *mekhala-choli*/blouse. These costumes as we see them today are the outcome of their evolution over nearly four thousand years of Indian history wrought with significant political, social and cultural upheavals. Consequently, costumes, which form an integral part of any historically dominant culture, too underwent crucial transformations.

The words presently used to designate costumes and clothing in India are *paridhana, vasha-bhusha* or *poshak* (in Hindi), or *libaas* (in Arabic). In the Vedic period, however, the word *paridhana* was used exclusively for the lower garment. (*Atharvaveda,* VIII, 2, 16)

The term 'costume' is derived from the Latin *consuetudo,* which means a complete set of outer garments, including ornaments and hairstyles. Costumes are used not only to cover the body and embellish it; they also constitute a significant non-verbal medium of communication that serves to establish the cultural identity of a person, including a person's community or country

Facing page:
Dancers and musicians in regal attire in the later Mughal court. Mid-19th century, Victoria and Albert Museum, London.

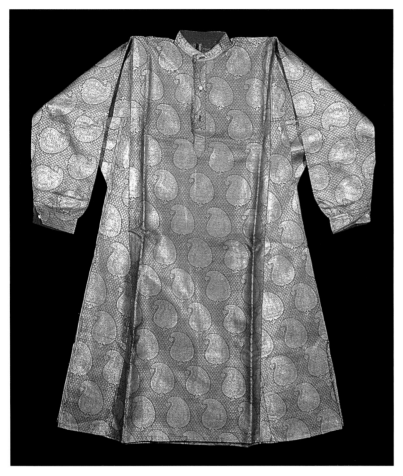

A brocade kurta, *Northern India. 20th century, National Museum, New Delhi.*

in different regions, as do the availability of raw material and the technical skills for creating fabrics that could be used to create the desired costumes. Besides these factors, social and economic status, as well as people's occupations determine the nature and quality of costumes that they are likely to wear.

The story of Indian costumes takes us on a journey back in time. India is the seventh largest country in the world, besides being the second most populous one. Situated entirely in the northern hemisphere, it covers a surface area of around 3,280,483 square kilometres with a varied landscape rich in biodiversity, spanning the mighty Himalayas along the north and the northeast; deserts in the west; and large coastal areas in the eastern, southeastern and southern parts of the country. Geographical factors have a direct bearing on climatic conditions, which in turn play a crucial role in the choice of material for the costumes of a particular region.

Apart from geographical and climatic parameters, over four thousand years of chequered history have contributed immensely to the evolution of Indian costumes, besides bequeathing to the country a rich and pluralistic cultural

of origin at any given historical period. They help understand fashion trends prevalent during a particular historical time-frame. It has been observed that fashion trends usually veer towards new directions every ten to twenty years.

Several factors—geographical, historical, religious, cultural—play a key role in determining the nature of costumes legacy. India was invaded several times (the Greeks, Sakas, Scythians, Kushans, Huns, the Sultanate, Khiljis, Lodis, Mughals, Europeans) from either the northwest or the south. Invaders like the Greeks and the Huns came to India in search of booty. They came, fought and sacked the country before departing with handsome loot. Innumerable warriors of invading armies, however, preferred staying on in the midst of the indigenous people, rather

than returning to their homeland. Other invaders conquered India and ruled over the indigenous people. In either case, a prolonged contact between the invader and the invaded led to a cultural exchange between the two—the logical outcome of the face-to-face interaction of culturally divergent peoples. These multi-cultural and ethnical influences have collectively and significantly altered and shaped Indian costumes as well.

Fairs, festivals and different religious ceremonies inspired weavers and artisans to create special religious costumes and textiles in India. Some of the popular religious costumes such as the *sadri*, *mirjai*, *kurta* or the *namavali chaddar*, have religious inscriptions either woven into them or printed on them.

Since the Vedic period, during ritualistic ceremonies draped garments were preferred to stitched ones. This tradition has been carried forward especially by priests in the southern part of India.

Apart from costumes associated with religious occasions, special ones are made for marriages in India, as elsewhere in the world. Traditional Indian marriages are lavish, colourful and elaborate as is evident from the concommitant costumes, jewellery, decoration and food. Myriad are the ethnic and regional variations in marriage costumes.

Motifs richly embroidered in a variety of threads have always added to the beauty of Indian costumes.

Therefore, Indian costumes present a dazzling array of shades and designs with their very own colour symbology, mesmerising people from all walks of life across the world.

An overview of Indian costumes from the Vedic times to the 20th century will help understand the vestimentary mosaic of India, with special focus on the prevalent vestimentary cultures of the Northern, Eastern and Northeastern, Western and Central, and Southern India. Each section attempts to present the history and traditions of the local costumes, and their variations according to occasions and social hierarchy—royalty, elite groups, soldiers, dancers, the common man, to name just a few, along with jewellery and other accessories.

According to some European scholars, Indian art barely depicts stitched garments, thereby perhaps implying that the indigenous people were not aware of stitching, and that stitching was an art taught by foreigners to the indigenous people. Tropical countries, however, have a history of people wearing loose and elegant garments in the form of a drape. Neither the sari nor the *dhoti* needs any stitching, but both are considered to be comfortable and graceful outfits. While art is an important index of the costumes of a society, it should not constitute the paramount yardstick to assess the vestimentary practices of a society during any particular historical period. Nudity, for instance, is a predominant theme in modern art, without being an index of any society's vestimentary practices. Indian art has essentially been inspired by religion, and religion has always laid great emphasis on the spiritual path to attain God. Even the well-known *Krishna-Leela*—Krishna stealing the costumes of the *gopi*s or cowherds—must be interpreted in a spiritual light. According to the Bhagvad Gita, the sacred Hindu text, to attain God one must rise above the world of attachment in one's purest form, and surrender oneself to God without hiding anything. In their

depiction of the *Krishna-Leela*, Indian miniaturists have conceived the pond as representing the earthly world of attachments in which the *gopi*s represent human beings who reach out for God without hiding anything from Him. Costumes are representative of the sins which the *gopi*s are wont to hide or cover up.

Indian art has always been a means for explaining the philosophical essence and ethos of Indian culture.

Three main sources—archaeological evidence, literary references and actual costumes—furnish crucial leads in the reconstruction of the history of Indian costumes. The archaeological history of Indian textiles starts from the Indus Civilisation (*c.* 2600-1400 BC). A plethora of literary references to costumes starts from the Vedic period (*c.* 1200-600 BC). The actual costumes in the museums and private collections abroad and in India date back to the 17th and 18th centuries. All these references provide interesting insights into the chronological and cultural trajectory described by Indian costumes through the ages.

INDUS CIVILISATION (C. 2600-1400 BC)

The Indus Civilisation, which was contemporaneous with the Chinese, Egyptian and Mesopotamian civilisations, flourished in the Northwestern part of undivided India, including present-day Pakistan and Bangladesh. Excavated remains of an agricultural society with a certain degree of specialisation in metallurgy, pottery, jewellery and textile-making, architecturally well-conceived dwellings and important trade links with contemporary civilisations, indicate that it was a well-developed civilisation, even in the third millennium BC. (Lal, 2002, 2-4)

The Indus Civilisation was fairly advanced in the art of textile-making as is evidenced by finds such as cotton seeds, cotton, silk and bast fibres and filaments, spindles, bobbins, needles, awls and other tools. (Mackey, 1931, 585-86; Kenoyer, 1998, 159) Terracotta and stone figurines unearthed from various excavation sites help understand the vestimentary trends of this era. From direct examples as well as detailed studies, it can be inferred that the typical dress both for men and women consisted of two pieces: a lower garment and an upper garment. The lower garment looked like the *dhoti*, while the upper garment, resembling a shawl, was taken under the right arm and over the left shoulder, leaving the right shoulder bare. Two stone sculptures indicative of men's clothing of this era – the bearded priest in a shawl (Karachi Museum, Pakistan) and the seated man sporting a cloak (Islamabad Museum, Pakistan) – have been found in Mohenjodaro. (Kenoyer, 1998, 215-16)

Besides draped garments, a few stone and terracotta sculptures of the Indus Civilisation indicate the use of stitched garments by the Indus people. A steatite seal from Mohenjodaro (Islamabad Museum, Pakistan) illustrates seven female figurines wearing long skirts/tunic-like garments. (Kenoyer, 1998, 193)

Finds of needles made of bone, ivory, iron and gold; and awls made of bone and ivory from almost all sites of the Indus Civilisation signify the possibility of some kind of stitching being practised during this period. (Pathak, 2000, 3-4)

Men usually wore their hair long, albeit styled in different ways, and sported either a hairband or a conical cap. Women had elegant coiffures and wore an elaborate fan-shaped head-dress. Sometimes women

The Bearded Priest (2600-1400 BC, Karachi Museum, Karachi) and the Dancing Girl of Mohenjodaro (2600-1400 BC, National Museum, New Delhi) provide evidence of Indian costumes and accessories from the Indus Civilisation.

13

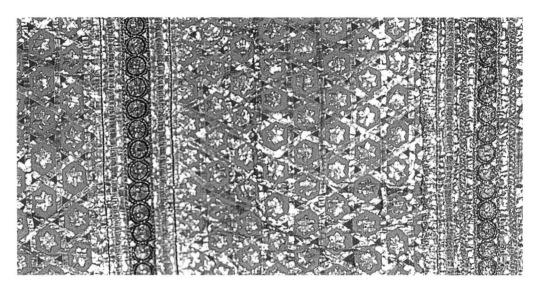

plaited their hair, as beautifully portrayed by the bronze dancing girl of Mohenjodaro. (Bhattacharya, 1985, 8)

Both men and women were fond of ornaments. Finds of necklaces, bangles and beads made of gold, silver, semi-precious stones and terracotta indicate the rich tradition of jewellery-making during the Indus Civilisation.

THE VEDIC PERIOD
(C. 1200-600 BC)

~

Vedic literature is the prime source of information on the Vedic period. This vast body of literature is associated with the Aryans, who resided in North India during the Vedic period. Vedic texts—the *Rig Veda*, *Sama Veda*, *Yajur Veda* and *Atharva Veda*, the *Brahmana*s and the *Upanishad*s— formed the bedrock of their culture and religion. These sources contain scant and widely dispersed notes about the everyday life of the people.

The Vedic people (the Aryans and the indigenous people) used *ksauma* (linen), *urnah* (wool), *dukala* (cotton) and animal skin to make garments. Garments for men consisted of three pieces: the *nivi* (lower garment), the *vasas* (upper garment) and the *adhivasa* (outer garment, shoulder cloth). The *usnisa* (turban) was added later. Garments for women consisted of two pieces: the *candataka* (under skirt) and the *vasas* (upper garment), while the *usnisa* is mentioned only in the context of goddesses. (Rau, 1989, 25) Besides these garments, there are references to sewn garments as well. The term *atka* is used for a long and close-fitting garment that was used by men. (*Rig Veda*, II, 35, 14; V, 74, 5) *Pesamsi* is a term often used for a pleated skirt (*Rig Veda*, I, 92, 4-5), artistically embroidered with gold and worn by dancers. The *darpi* was a close-fitting gold-embroidered vest worn by men and women of social standing. (*Rig Veda*, I, 166, 10; I 25, 13; IX, 100, 9) The king tied his turban at the *Rajasuya* and *Vajapeya* sacrifices in a manner where the ends were gathered together and tucked in front. (*Satapatha Brahmana*, 3.5.20) The *Rajasuya*

sacrifice was performed by a king to mark his having subdued all other kings, whereas the *Vajapeya* sacrifice, which conferred paramount sovereignty on the performer, could also be performed by a Brahmin.

There is a reference to a drape, in the *Sabha Parv* of the epic Mahabharata, in which Draupadi's *chirharan* (disrobing), the watershed episode of the Mahabharata, has been mentioned. According to this reference, Draupadi's sari was extended by Lord Krishna, when Dushasana tried to pull it off in the court of the Kaurava king of Hastinapur, Dhritarashtra. In the Ramayana, Sita asks for the golden deer to make garments from its skin. Such a reference indicates that queens

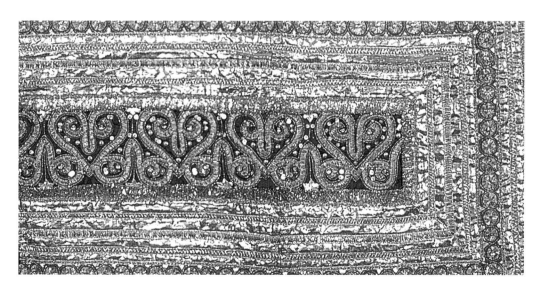

Visible in the sandstone sculpture of the dampati *(couple) are the finer details of the drapery. Stylised hairdo and jewellery enhance the couple's charm. 2nd century BC, National Museum, New Delhi.*

too were well versed in the art of stitching.

Necklaces, armlets, head ornaments and earrings were the usual ornaments worn by men and women of the Vedic period. (Majumdar, 1988, 397) The early *Samhita*s do not mention footwear. The first confirmed term for a shoe, *upanah*, appeared in the *Samhita*s (*Taittireya Samhita*, V. 4.4.4), the *Veda*s (*Atharva Veda*, XX 133, 4) and the *Brahmana*s (*Satapatha Brahmana*, V, 4, 3, 19). The *Satapatha Brahmana* mentions that sandals or shoes were made of boar skin, and were to be worn only on religious occasions.

THE MAURYA AND SUNGA PERIODS (C. 324-72 BC)

Chandragupta Maurya (324-300 BC) founded the first consolidated empire in India, controlling the Indus and the Ganges plains, and farther northwest. Megasthenes, the Seleucid ambassador at the Mauryan court and author of *Indika*, provides valuable information about the Mauryan court and its activities. Chandragupta Maurya's minister Kautilya (also known as Chanakya) had written the *Arthashastra*, the most elaborate document on the political, economic and social conditions of this period. Chandragupta Maurya's grandson Asoka (274-237 BC) was one of India's greatest rulers, and had close religious links with Central Asia and China.

Pushyamitra Sunga (187-151 BC), an

official under the declining Mauryas, was the founder of the Sunga Empire, which extended from Magadha (present-day Bihar) to Malwa (Central India). Patanjali's grammar was written during this period. Sculptures of the Sanchi and Bharhut stupas (Madhya Pradesh), and other stupas in Patna (Bihar) and Pitalkora (Deccan) provide fine examples of garments and costumes worn by kings, commoners and *bhikku*s, or Buddhist monks. (Chandra, 1973, 17-18)

This period of Indian history is important as it provides evidence of a mélange of foreign and indigenous garments. The literature of this period—Megasthenes' *Indika*, Kautilya's *Arthashastra*, parts of the *Sabha Parva* of the Mahabharata—mentions that cotton, wool, linen and *valkala* (animal skin) were used for garments by the people of the Maurya and Sunga periods. A stone panel from Bharhut, dating back to the Sunga period, depicts two men wearing garments made of leaves. From the sculpture of this period, it appears that men and women continued to wear three-piece unstitched garments: *antariya* (lower garment), *uttariya* (upper garment), and *kayaband* (waistband). (Alkazi, 1983, 21) That women tied the *antariya* in a variety

This sandstone railing pillar depicts a salbhanjika *(bearer of the* sal *tree branch) wearing a very ornate and heavy necklace and girdle, her hair falling in a long and neat braid. 2nd century* BC, *National Museum, New Delhi.*

of styles is evidenced by the sculptures as well. One such example is the sculpture of a *yakshi* or *chauri-* (sacred fly whisk) bearer found in Didarganj. (Patna Museum, Bihar) It depicts the *yakshi* wearing a *dhoti* that reaches down to the ankles, and is secured at the waist with a five-stringed girdle. She is elegantly bejewelled as well.

Sewn garments were also in vogue by this time and used by Persian soldiers: their typical costume was a sleeved tunic with crossed straps on the chest to carry the quiver, and a leather belt to carry the sword. The lower garment was more often the Indian *antariya* than the Persian trousers. Conical caps were more popular among the Persians.

The garment of the *bhikkus* consisted of three pieces: *sanghati, antarvasaka* and *uttarasanga. Bhikkunis* or Buddhist nuns were allowed to use the *kancuka*, apart from garments similar to those worn by the *bhikkus*.

Men and women used ornamental, elaborate and stylish headdresses, as is evident from the sculptures of this period. These sculptures show a wide variety of jewellery: necklaces, earrings, armlets, bracelets and belts, among others, that both men and women wore ordinarily. (Alkazi, 1983, 23) The bun-shaped, string-decorated hairdo of the Didarganj *yakshi* along with her necklaces, bangles and anklets, provides a fine idea of the jewellery of the Maurya and Sunga periods. Jewellery die made of black stone with beautiful floral patterns, similar to those found in the sculptures of this period, (Bahmania, 1994, 69) have been found in North India. (Sunga Period, 1st century BC-1st century AD). Shoes and sandals of different shapes, colours and materials formed an integral part of the people's vestimentary habits.

THE SATAVAHANA PERIOD (C. 200 BC-AD 250)

~

The Satavahana, or Andhra, Empire was established in the Deccan when the Mauryan Empire was in the final stages of its decline. The Satavahana Empire touched new heights under the reign of Gautamiputra Satakarni (r. *c.* AD 106-130) and Vashishiputra Pulamayi (r. *c.* AD 130-159). This was a peaceful period, and trade and industry flourished well in the domestic and overseas markets. The indigenous people were influenced by the Romans, which is well-reflected in the marvellously sculpted gateways of the Sanchi Stupa (Madhya Pradesh), in

Buddha is depicted here, dressed in chequered cloth. 2nd century AD, sandstone, Government Museum, Mathura.

Ajanta (cave numbers IX, X, Aurangabad, Maharashtra), at Amaravati and Nagarjunkonda (South India), and in other monuments of this period.

This phase was marked by the continuity of the earlier kinds of garments, except there were more variations in the wearing styles. The indigenous dress constituted four pieces: *uttariya, antariya, kayaband* and *usnisa*. Attendants, hunters and military personnel, however, wore a stitched shirt-like garment resembling a tunic. Monks and ascetics wore clothes made of rags patched together and dyed reddish yellow. (Sivaramamurti, 1977, 103, pl. VIII)

During the reign of the Satavahanas, men usually wore *dhoti*s that reached down to the knees; one end of the *dhoti* was tucked at the back and the other gathered in folds and tucked in the front. The *dhoti* was secured at the waist with a *kamarband* tied into a bow-shaped knot. As portrayed in the sculptures of this period, the upper part of the body was usually depicted bare. Men did, however, wear turbans and scarves in different styles.

Women of this period are represented wearing two types of lower garments (Chandra, 1973, 21): one end of a narrow scarf is attached to the girdle and the other tucked behind, or one end of the loin-cloth reaching down to the knee is wrapped round the waist, and the other end is pleated and tucked in front and passed between the legs. Sometimes women wore *kamarband*s as well, and usually covered their heads with decorative *odhani*s or turbans. During this period footwear was made of boar or deer skin. As portrayed in the stone sculptures of this period, the indigenous people wore much more jewellery than the foreigners; their headgear and hairstyles were also very fancy and elaborate. (Alkazi, 1983, 72-73) Men wore turbans, while women preferred to sport their hair in a bun.

THE KUSHAN PERIOD
(C. 130 BC-AD 185)

~

In the history of Indian costumes, the Kushan period is considered to be one of the most important ones. There was no uniformity in the costumes of this period, and these varied from region to region. The Kushan rulers, who basically belonged to the Turkish tribe Yueh-chi, ruled for almost three centuries. This period was significant on the political and economic fronts. On the political front the Kushans ruled across Northern and Central India from 130 BC to AD 185. Before them Bactrican Greeks ruled Gandhara, Taxshila and Kabul Valley; and the Sakas and Parthians ruled Mathura, Taxshila, Malwa, and the Kathiawar Peninsula. Economically this phase witnessed the development of the Central Asian trade routes. As a result, communication

between parts of India and other countries improved, influencing the indigenous costumes and lifestyles. Many foreigners and their garments were very alluring and intriguing for the indigenous people. With slight modification, the costumes of the foreigners were accepted by royalty, the army personnel, dancers and other elite groups. This has been well depicted in the stone, terracotta and ivory sculptures of this period unearthed from sites at Gandhara, Mathura, Taxshila, Besnagar and Begram. (Banerjee, 1956; Sharma, 1995; Marshall, 1951)

The Gandhara School of art is influenced by the Greeks and Romans, while the Mathura School of art was a direct continuation of the native Indian schools of Bharhut and Sanchi.

Literary texts—especially on the Buddhist *Tripitaka*s, the Jain canon and Sanskrit literature—throw light on the types of garments worn during these times, detailing textures and the use of different materials. These are also important records of

The soapstone Gandhara Buddha is renowned for its fine and free-flowing sanghati *(robe). 2nd century* AD, *National Museum, New Delhi.*

21

the various techniques of embellishments on the garments including exquisite embroidery with thread or pearl.

An important discovery of a group of portrait statues of Kanishka (r. *c.* AD 78-101 or 102), Vima-Kadphises (r. *c.* AD 65-75), and Kushan Satrap Chashtan (r. *c.* AD 130-131, ruler of Sind who ruled jointly with his grandson Raja Rudradaman) from Mathura, Uttar Pradesh, provides valuable information about the costumes of the Kushan rulers. In these sculptures the Kushan emperor has been shown in typical Kushan-style clothes – heavy and severe, stiff and formal. These consisted of a long padded coat/tunic, loose or fitting trousers, riding boots and pointed caps. It appears that since the Kushans never looked upon India as their home, they probably either preferred only Central Asian costumes or it may be that these sculptures constituted an official representation of the ruler.

After the royal and elite groups, the next important social constituency comprised soldiers. Kushan sculptures illustrate two styles of soldiers' costumes— the indigenous group wearing the 'loincloth, waistband and scarf/turban'; and the foreign group wearing the 'helmet, armour of the Assyrian type or the shirt, *dhoti*, turban.'

This period was marked by an equally rich variety of drapes and stitched costumes for women. In the Gandhara School, women have been shown in a sari-type attire consisting mainly of the *kamarband* and *chaddar/dupatta*. The Mathura School is typified by the sari/skirt and the *kamarband*, with or without the *dupatta*. A fascinating aspect is the variations in wearing style in both the schools. Listed below are some of the popular wearing styles:

1. Sleeved tunic, a sort of petticoat and shawl/scarf.
2. Sari-type attire with *kamarband* and *chaddar/dupatta*, which seems to have evolved from the Roman attire. It appears that there were two to three ways of wrapping and pleating the sari-like attire.
3. Foreign women are usually depicted

in a tunic, pleated skirt and a *kamarband*.

4. Sometimes the foreigners wear a loose *kamarband* and a *chaddar* or *dupatta*.

The Mathura sculptures also depict a variety of women's garments:

1. Sari with or without *dupatta* and *kamarband*.
2. Skirts worn by women in some of the sculptures.
3. Tunics in which foreign women were sometimes depicted.

*Bhikku*s or Buddhist monks continued to wear rugged clothes or garments made of barks, leaves, or animal skin. The *Patimokkha Sutta* of the *Vinaya Pitaka* mentions that there were several rules to follow while dyeing the *civara*s (*vastra* or cloth), drying dyed cloth, and dividing and distributing the *civara*s among and to the recipients. (*Mahavagga,* VIII, 5-9) Two Gandhara sculptures depict ascetics, wearing half *dhoti*s up to their knees, while their upper portion is bare. Some of them do wear an upper garment—a piece of cloth taken under the right armpit and tied over the left shoulder. (Maxwell, 1982, 167)

The Sangam literature of the South also provides references to the vestimentary traditions prevalent in Southern India from the 1st century BC to the 4th century AD. Sculptures of Amaravati, Nagarjunkonda and Golli also throw light on the contemporaneous social life of South India. These sculptures depict the common man wearing a *dhoti*/loincloth, *kamarband* and turban. The *dhoti* and *kamarband* were worn in two or three different styles. The *chaddar* or *dupatta* was not very common, but the turban was also a part of South Indian men's attire. Royalty and noblemen usually wore tunics. Sometimes attendants, army personnel and musicians also wore tunics with tight-fitting full sleeves. A stone panel from Nagarjunkonda depicts a guard on either side. One of them is dressed in the indigenous *dhoti*, while the other one wears the foreigner's attire—tunic, trousers and

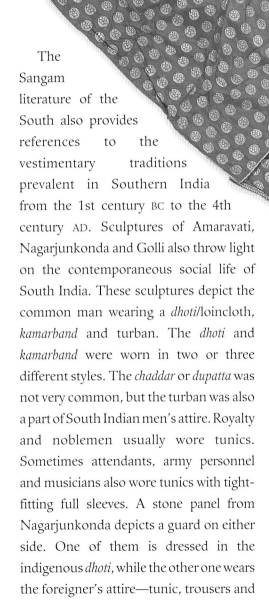

Detail of a quilted brocade jama *from Rajasthan. 19th century, National Museum, New Delhi.*

23

This soapstone pillar depicts a palace guardian in a tunic, paijama *and shoes that are in keeping with his profession and social standing. 3rd century* AD, *National Museum, New Delhi.*

probably on ceremonial occasions, they wore turbans. (Chandra, 1973, 44)

Excavation findings of gold necklaces, bracelets, bangles, earrings and rings from Taxshila constitute a very important discovery. (Asthana, 1985, 225-26). The elegant designs, intricate carvings and fine workmanship of these jewellery pieces bear testimony to the highly skilled craft of jewellery-making of that period. While the Greco-Roman style dominates the patterns, a few Indian decorative designs were also used in the jewellery of these times. Often, semi-precious stones were used in some of these pieces.

THE GUPTA PERIOD (C. AD 4TH-5TH CENTURIES)

~

The Gupta Empire started in AD 320 with the accession of Chandragupta I, who ruled till AD 340 over the petty kingdom of Magadha (including Bengal). His son Samudragupta (r. AD 340-380) and grandson Chandragupta Vikramaditya (r. AD 380-415) took the Gupta Empire to its zenith: this phase is known as the Golden Age in Indian history.

a cap in the manner of a Scythian solider.

Women in Southern India wore a sari, a *kamarband* and a scarf. Usually women did not wear headdresses, but arranged their hair in diverse coiffures. At times,

The Golden Age is notable for its fine balance and harmony in all arts, be that literature, music, numismatics, costumes, or textiles.

Rich Sanskrit literature (*Amarkosh* by Amarsingh, *Sankuntala*, *Raghuvamsa* and *Kumarasambhava* by Kalidas, *Mahavira-Charita* and *Uttarrama-Charita* by Bhavabhuti), the travel accounts of the Chinese Buddhist monk Fa-Hien, and epigraphic evidences provide a range of information on textiles and costumes. These refer not only to the use of a variety of cotton, silk and wool, but also to their quality, texture and production centres. These literary evidences help in understanding the visual depiction in the Ajanta, Ellora and Bagh murals. Another important source of information on the Gupta period is its coinage, which throws light on the royal attire worn by the Gupta rulers. It is clear from the coins of this period that the Gupta rulers wore stitched garments, and perhaps the elite group did so, too. Gold coins from Samudragupta's reign depict him wearing a tunic, trousers and a cap. Often, the Gupta rulers have been shown in calf-length tunics and loose trousers.

The costumes of the Parthian-Kushan rulers varied from quilted and padded coats to *kurta*s with sleeves and slits on the sides, and trousers. Apart from stitched garments, indigenous costumes *(antariya, uttariya* and *kamarband)* were equally popular. In Cave no. 6 of Ajanta is the painting of a monk wearing a short *dhoti*. A *kamarband* is wrapped around the upper portion and taken over the left shoulder. (Ghosh, 1967, pl. 1) On the ceiling decoration of Cave no. 1, a distinguished foreigner (a Persian perhaps) enjoys his

In this sandstone sculpture, the dancer in the middle is distinct in her attire from the four musicians who flank her. 5th century AD, National Museum, New Delhi.

A sandstone depiction of Krishna overturning a cart with Yashodhara clad in a long tunic and flared paijama, *watching him. 5th century* AD, *National Museum, New Delhi.*

drink along with his attendants. He is dressed in a long, tight-fitting and full-sleeved tunic, a conical cap, a scarf and a waistband. The attendant to his right is wearing a skirt-like lower garment with frills. The attendant to his left is wearing a full-length, full-sleeved *jama* with a V-shaped opening at the neck, and a skullcap.

In Cave no. 1 figures the *Sankhapala Jataka* depicts kings and other members of the nobility, wearing an *antariya* of fine silk or muslin along with the *kanchuka*, tucked in like a shirt. A *kayaband* was used at the waist to hold the garments in place. Turbans were worn mainly by certain dignitaries, ministers and other important officials.

By this period a change in the base material was noticeable. Instead of the earlier heavy and padded tunic, people now started using lighter material. Transparent and lighter textures or materials are mentioned in literature, and are evident even in the stone sculptures. Garments were embellished using different techniques—embroidering them with beads in colourful flora-fauna patterning with flower-dyed thread.

A study of the Ajanta paintings reveals a plethora of women's costumes such as the sari, *ghagra* and *choli*, to name a few, and their wearing styles. Roshan Alkazi has done a masterly stylistic evaluation of women's garments. She mentions that the *antariya* could be worn in several different ways (Alkazi, 1983,147):

1. In the *kachcha* style, the *dhoti* was worn as the *ghagra*, first wrapped around the

right hip, then around the body and tucked in at the left hip.

2. In the second category, the *kachcha* and *ghagra* were worn together with a short *antariya* or *calanika*. In this style, the attire was drawn up first in the *kachcha* style and the longer end then wrapped around like a short *ghagra*.

It has been observed that the ankle-length *antariya* was worn by the nobility, and the shorter one by the attendants. Sometimes the *antariya* was worn like the Indonesian sarong. It appears that the *kachcha* style of the *antariya* was gradually replaced by the *ghagra* or *lungi* among dancers and the common man, although elite groups remained conservative in their taste. Besides these draped costumes, stitched garments were also worn during this period. A stone panel from Deogarh depicts Devaki, Krishna's mother, wearing trousers and a *choli/kurta* with an apron in front. Another example shows dancers wearing short skirts with a zig-zag instead of a straight hemline. One of the stone sculptures housed in the Bikaner Museum depicts a lady wearing a *ghagra*. (Bhandari, 2004, 15)

The breast band had been used since the Vedic period. Sanskrit literature mentions a stitched garment variously known as the '*cholaka, chola, choli, cholika, kancholika*'. One of the earliest visual references of the *choli* appears in a painting in Cave no. 1 of Ajanta – of the *Mahajanaka Jataka*, in which the dancer is wearing a full-sleeved, tight-fitting *choli* with an

Enamelled kangan*s (bangles) with elephant-head clasps continue to be a part of an Indian woman's accessories. 19th century, Roli Books Collection.*

27

Harshacharita:
Rich in Textile References

~

*H*arshacharita is a landmark text of ancient Indian history, and presents an elaborate description of the social and cultural life of North India of the 6th-7th centuries. Written by Banabhatta, the court poet of Emperor Harshavardhana of Kanauj, Uttar Pradesh, *Harshacharita* is a fascinating account of Emperor Harshavardhana's life and his courtly activities, and abounds in references to textiles and costumes of the time. Banabhatta mentions that Emperor Harshavardhana used to wear two main garments: the *antariya* and the *uttariya*, a silk *patka* around the waist and a girdle over it. The *uttariya* was made of fine cloth textured like a *jamdani*. The emperor and the common man both wore necklaces and head ornaments. (Agrawala, 1963, 46)

Banabhatta mentions six types of materials used for making garments during this period. These included different qualities of cotton, silk and linen. While describing the wedding of Rajshri, the emperor's sister, Banabhatta mentions that Bhaskarvarman, the ruler of Assam, and a contemporary of Emperor Harshavardhana, presented her with silk from Assam as his special gift.

Banabhatta further elaborates on four types of coats: the *kanchuk* (long, full-sleeved coat with covered neck), the *barban* (similar to the *kanchuk*, but shorter in length), the *chincholaka* (loose, long, front-open *chola* to be worn over the *kanchuk* like a *choga*), and the *kuparsak* (about the same length as the *chola*, and sleeveless like a waistcoat). Three types of *paijama*s were prevalent during Emperor Harshavardhana's reign: the *suthan* (tight-fitting

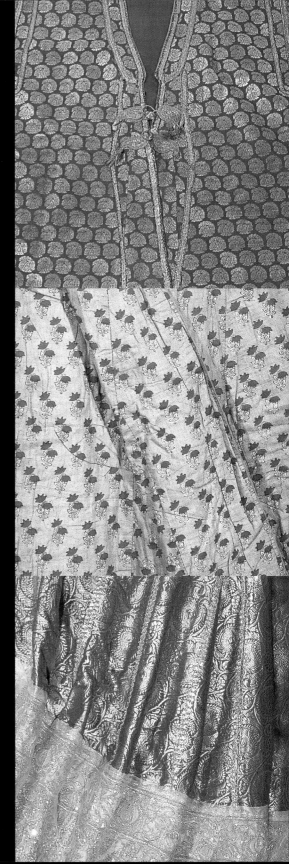

lower garment); the *pinga* (loose *salwar*); and the *sthula* (short *paijama*s or shorts). These were particularly used by the royals. The popular attire of the women of this period was the sari and the *chaddar*. (Agrawala, 1963, 151)

These textiles and costumes were embellished in a variety of ways: *chuntdar* (*chunt* means 'pleats' and *chuntdar* refers to costumes with pleats as well as to the person who practices this art), *bandhej* (tie and dye), pearl-embroidered, or block-printed. Banabhatta mentions that servants were specifically engaged for doing *chunt*s especially on the *uttariya*. After the *chunt*s were done, an attire was always kept pleated. (Agrawala, 1963, 76) He also mentions that women were experts in making designs for *bandhej*, dyeing and printing. (Agrawala, 1963, 74-75) Besides these, he refers to pearl-embroidered costumes as well.

The *Harshacharita* is replete with information on other textiles and costumes, thereby corroborating the rich textile tradition and the refined aesthetic taste of people around the 6th-7th centuries. (Agrawala, 1963, 80)

India has one of the largest varieties of textiles in the world, making it a much-sought-after destination for fashion gurus the world over. Till date Indian cottons and silks remain unparalleled in their texture and appeal.

apron in front. (Ghosh, 1967, pl. IX) A somewhat similar kind of *choli* is still worn by the women of Rajputana and Baluchistan. These *choli*s were either simple breast coverings or sometimes featured an additional apron-like attachment in front.

Apart from the sari, *ghagra* and *choli*, another very important costume depicted in art is the *kurta* or the Persian shirt. These *kurta*s have an opening at the neck and slits on the sides. Some of the women's *kurta*s have slits on the sides and give the

importance of this skill. In sculptures people have been shown in indigenous costumes and sporting long hair arranged in different styles:

a) A bun worn either high or low on the nape of the neck;
b) A bun knotted to the side of the head;
c) Hair wound to the left on top of the head.

Sometimes these hairstyles were decorated with pearl string or flowers.

In the Ajanta paintings men have been

impression of a four-pointed hemline. Another style of the *kurta* was with a crossover flap and side openings, somewhat similar to the *angarkha*. The ankle-length fitted tunics appear to be of the Turanian Tartar style.

Elaborate hairstyles were in fashion during the Gupta period. Mention of Sandhari (Draupadi's name during her period of exile in the Mahabharata) as an expert in hairdressing highlights the

depicted wearing turbans, while in coins emperors have been portrayed in the Kushan-Parthian attire wearing a skullcap or headgear. This could well have been the military or sports dress. It appears that a crown with a band embellished with pearls and garlands replaced the turban during the Gupta period, especially with royalty. Evidence corroborates that the costumes of the Gupta period were indeed remarkable in style, cut and colour.

POST-GUPTA PERIOD (7TH-12TH CENTURIES)

~

The post-Gupta period was essentially a phase of power struggle among provinces and feudatory states. It was also a period that witnessed repeated attacks of the Huns which weakened North India. The important ruler of the North in the post-Gupta era was Harshavardhana (r. AD 606-646), whose court poet Banabhatta wrote the *Harshacharita*. He gives an elaborate garment. (Agrawala, 1963, 80) This shows the variation in the costumes of this period. He does not, however, discuss any of the costumes except the *kanchuka*, which makes it difficult to understand the style and shape of the other garments. The *kanchuka* is a long, full-sleeved, coat-like attire coming almost up to the knee. Besides these, the sari, *dhoti* and *odhani* were other costumes worn by women described by Banabhatta while detailing the marriage of Rajshri, Harshavardhana's sister. (Agrawala, 1963, 74-84) After

The five Cosmic Buddhas preceding the four Vajrayana deities are depicted in the traditional Buddhist sanghati *(robe). c. 1100, Bharat Kala Bhawan, Benaras.*

description of the courtly activities, and, interestingly, talks about the costumes, prevalent fashion trends, and materials used for costumes. He mentions that Harsha usually wore a three-piece attire: the *antariya* or *dhoti*, the *uttariya* and the *patka*, along with head ornaments and earrings, among other accessories. (Agrawala, 1963, 46-47) While describing the royal attire, Banabhatta uses the terms *kanchuka*, *varban*, *chincholak* and *kuparsak* for the upper

Harshavardhana, the Pala (in Bihar), Gujarat-Pratihara (in Western India) and Chalukyan (in Deccan) dynasties fought for the seat of power. Around 916, the Gujarat-Pratihara Empire showed signs of weakening and soon North India was divided into numerous petty states. Around the 12th century, the standards of Islam were firmly planted in North India.

The period between 700 and 1200 was wrought with political instability.

Therefore, vestimentary evidence of this phase is drawn more from literary sources than from works of art. Sanskrit, Arabic, Persian and vernacular literature are replete with references to costumes, but in the absence of good commentaries in Arabic and Persian literature, sometimes it becomes difficult to interpret the terms denoting certain fabrics. Another problem is that often textiles and costumes were named after localities without any mention of technique, style and utility. Chinese and Arab geographers described in detail the textile trade and production centres, and, at times, designs, colours, materials and costumes used by the elite groups and the common man.

The literature of the post-Gupta period mentions cotton, silk and wool. Men usually wore a tunic, trousers, and a turban. Stone and terracotta sculptures, and palm-leaf paintings of Vajrayana Buddhism of this period indicate that the indigenous attire (*antariya*, *uttariya*, *kamarband*, crown or turban) was also worn by the people. Women wore long tunics, upper garments, sleeved bodices and the *uttariya*. Necklaces, earrings, bangles, girdles and rings were the basic jewellery worn during this period. Numerous Pala sculptures depict the jewellery tradition. One such example is the stone sculpture of Tara. Her lower garment has soft and delicate folds. She also wears some accessories: a broad necklace tightly fitted around the neck, a beaded long necklace, armlets and a girdle. (Bahmania, 1994, 68)

THE PALLAVAS (7TH-9TH CENTURIES)

~

The Pallavas of Kanchi represent an early dynasty in South India. Simhavishnu (r. last quarter of the 6th century AD), Mahendravarman I (r. *c.* AD 600-630), Narasimhavarman I (r. *c.* AD 630-638) and Rajasimha (r. AD 740-765) were the famous kings of the Pallava Dynasty. They contributed immensely towards the construction of rock-cut temples at Mahabalipuram and Mamandur, the Kailasanatha Temple at Kanchipuram, and temples at Panamalai. The

Kailasanatha Temple is a splendid example of the Pallava phase of painting and stone sculpture. One of the Panamalai temple paintings depicts a goddess wearing a *dhoti* with floral patterns, crowns, necklaces and heavy girdles, depicting the trends of costumes and jewellery prevalent during the Pallava period. (Sivaramamurti, 1968, 62)

THE CHOLAS (9TH-13TH CENTURIES)

~

In the 9th century, the Cholas regained power when Vijaylasya (r. AD 850-871) established his rule in the area around Tanjavur. Aditya (r. AD 871-907), Parantaka (r. AD 907-953), Gandaradaitya (r. AD 953-957), Rajaraja (r. AD 985-1016) and Rajendra (r. AD 1012-44) were great Chola temple builders. The widowed queen of Gandaradaitya, Sembiyan Mahadevi, was one of the most important Chola queens who upheld the generous tradition of building and endowing temples. One of the most important monuments of the Chola period is the Rajarajesvaram Temple at Tanjavur, also known as the Brihadisvara Temple.

King Siddhartha with messengers in formal attire. 15th century, National Museum, New Delhi.

Facing page:
Shah Jahan in his typical and stylised Shah Jahani turban, jama, paijama *and* patka. *17th century* AD, *Victoria and Albert Museum, London.*

The paintings of the Brihadisvara Temple constitute the most valuable document on painting as an art during this period. On the walls of the Brihadisvara Temple are three prostrated heavenly musicians, two female and one male. All of them are wearing the lower garment with heavy girdles and the usual jewellery. The female musicians have done up their hair in a heavy bun, while the male has a crown-like hairdo. (Sivaramamurti, 1968, 82-83) Chola bronzes and stone sculptures are most intricately carved, beautifully illustrating

the fancy hairstyles and ornamented lower garments.

PRE-MUGHAL PERIOD (13TH-15TH CENTURIES)

~

The 10th century onwards, North India was subjected to several attacks by Mahmud of Ghazni and Muhammad Ghori, mainly because of the feeble emperors of that region. The invaders did not stay in India and returned to their homeland with booty.

Several Muslim dynasties occupied the seat of power in Delhi and ruled India before the Mughals. The important ones, however, are the Mamluk Sultans (r. 1192-1298); the Khaljis (r. 1290-1320); the Tughlaqs (r. 1320-1414); the Sayyids (r. 1440-51) and the Lodhis (r. 1451-1526). The Sultanate of Delhi came to an end in 1526, when Babur defeated Ibrahim Lodhi and laid the foundation of the Mughal Empire. Nevertheless, Mughal rule was firmly established only during Humayun's reign (r. 1530-40 and 1555-56).

The ambience at the pre-Mughal court of the Muslim Sultans was characterised by intense religious fervour. This period witnessed the intermingling of two cultural sensibilities – the indigenous and the Islamic. This influenced the art and culture of this period, as reflected in the two contemporaneous schools of art (indigenous and Persian). The indigenous school of painting was dominated by the Western Indian tradition, while the Islamic school was directly influenced by the Persian style. Paintings of both these styles are an invaluable index of the distinct costumes used by men and women of this period. Western Indian Jain manuscripts (*Laur Chanda*, *Aranyaka Parva*, *Mandu Kalpasutra* and *Devi Mahatmya*), although mainly religious texts, are a valuable source of information on the costumes of the people. In these paintings men have been portrayed in a full-sleeved *kurta-/jama*-like garment, popularly know as the *chakdar jama*, with slits at the sides ending in four pointed ends instead of a straight hemline, with fastenings to the right or left, a *paijama* and a *kamarband*. These costumes were probably made of fine cotton, as they appear to be transparent.

Under the new sultanate emerged a new style of painting and architecture, known as the Sultanate Style. This style was shaped by three preponderant

influences: the patrons' cultural origins in Iran, Afghanistan and Central India. The result was a syncretism—the interpretation of the Iranian styles through the prism of Indian tradition. The *choga*, *jama* and *paijama* constituted men's attire. The Afghan skullcap tied with a turban is another predominant male sartorial feature. Women have been shown in patterned *ghagra*s, tight *choli*s and diaphanous and stiff *odhani*s.

Besides visual representations, literature has provided important clues to costumes. A Muslim writer, Qalaqushandi, records in *Subh-ul-Asa* the attire of the Sultans, Khans, Maliks, soldiers and other officers. He says that they wore '*tatariyat*s (gowns), *jakalwat*s (probably a type of gown) and Islamic *qaba*s (full-sleeved outer garment worn by men) of *khwarizm* tucked in at the waist and short turbans that did not exceed five or six forearms.' Sultan Firoz Shah Tughlaq and his courtiers wore different kinds of dresses. The Sultan himself is said to have worn a *kulah* (skullcap) that cost a *lakh* of *tanka* (currency prevalent during the medieval period). (Afif, 1890, 48) Amir Khusrau explained the word *barani* as some sort of overcoat. Firoz Shah Tughlaq used to wear a *barani*—a woollen or silken coat with embroidered sleeves. (Chandra, 1973; 144)

THE MUGHAL PERIOD (16TH-19TH CENTURIES)

Zahir-ud-din Mohammad Babur (r. 1526-30), a descendant of Timur of Samarkand from his father's side and of Chingiz Khan's clan from his mother's side, founded the Mughal Empire in AD 1526 by defeating Ibrahim Lodhi in the first Battle of Panipat. Each Mughal ruler – Humayun (r. 1530-40 and 1555-56), Akbar (r. 1556-1605), Jahangir (r. 1605-28), Shah Jahan (r. 1628-58), Aurangzeb (r. 1658-1707) and the later Mughals (1707-1857) – left a distinct mark in every conceivable field of art, culture and lifestyle. This period of Indian history is well recorded in the literature, architecture, paintings, costumes and jewellery of the time. Numerous miniature paintings that are today the prized possessions of museums and private collections the world over, were executed during the Mughal period. These miniature paintings also provide a useful window to life under the Mughals. The emperor's

Facing page:
Shan Jahan receives his three sons, princes Dara Shikoh, Shah Shaja and Aurangzeb, on March 8, 1628. Musicians and courtiers alike are clad in their finest costumes. Padshahnama, c. *1640.* The Royal Collection © 2006, Her Majesty Queen Elizabeth II.

Imperial Wardrobe

~

Abu'l Fazl Allami's *Ain-i-Akbari*, the third volume of the *Akbarnama*, gives a full account of Akbar's reign covering in detail its cultural and economic highlights. It provides interesting insights into the *karkhana*s or manufacturing units, and the *tohshkhana*s or treasure houses, and the way they functioned. Under the Mughals, all sorts of royal robes for personal use and for the *khilat* (robe of honour) were made in the imperial *karkhana*s, and stored in the *tohshkhana*s. *Karkhana*s were established at Lahore, Agra, Fatehpur, Ahmedabad and Gujarat to take care of all sorts of imperial needs, be it costume jewellery, footwear, or other accessories. And the *tohshkhana*s were used to store these articles.

It is evident from the records that an elaborate storing system was in place during this period. The *Ain-i-Akbari* mentions:

> Each year a thousand costumes were made for the Imperial Wardrobe and hundred and twenty of these were always kept ready for the emperor... The Imperial Wardrobe was arranged according to the day, month and year. Each and every garment was arranged according to its colour, price

---

Zari brocade choga *used by the elite of the Northern region. 19th century, National Museum, New Delhi.*

and weight. This arrangement was called *misl*, a set. All articles that were bought, woven to order, or received as tributes or presents, were carefully preserved, and according to the order in which they were preserved, they were again taken out for inspection, or given out to be cut and made up, or given away as presents. Articles that arrived at the same time were arranged according to their prices.

Clerks used to maintain records very meticulously. They used to arrange the costumes and accessories the emperor was to wear according to norms that prescribed wearing certain costumes on certain days, and an entry was made in the *bahi*s (record books). The following day the same set would be returned to the clerks, who would then delete the entry from the *bahi*s before giving out a new set of clothes for the emperor. The *Ain-i-Akbari* further states, 'The clerks used to fix or store the garments according to details of every article worn, which they would write on a strip of cloth and attach to the end of the pieces. The following is the order of colour: ruby-coloured, golden, orange, brass-coloured, crimson, grass-green, cotton flower-coloured, sandalwood-coloured, almond-coloured, purple, grape...'

(*Ain-i-Akbari*, Abu'l Fazl Allami,
tr. H. Blochmann, 1965, 97)

On special occasions Indian royalty can still be seen in costumes that recall an opulent past. Roli Books Collection.

courtly activities, however, take a clear thematic precedence over the common man's life in these paintings. Foreign travellers from European countries who visited India from the 16th century onwards, provide a much wider range of information on the common man in their accounts and works.

Costumes worn by Babur and his courtiers resembled those of his country of origin, while the common man during Babur's reign continued to wear indigenous costumes, as Babur himself mentioned in the *Baburnama*. The common man wore a short wrap-around *dhoti*, while the upper portion was left bare. Babur also refers to the names of a few costumes, Turkish or Mongol perhaps, some of which are listed below:

Nimcha (kind of short tunic); *jama* (garment with lining); *yaktahi jama* (garment without lining); *charqab* (gold-embroidered garment); *postin* or coat (lined with sheepskin); *jiba* or *surtout*; *chafan* (long coat); and *tahband* (girdle or belt).

(Goswamy, 1993, 14)

Costumes from Humayun's reign were almost like those from Babur's – *qaba*, *jama*, *pirahan*, *jilucha*, *jiba* and *kasaba*, to name a few. Very few paintings detailing costumes from Babur's and Humayun's reigns have survived. In fact, in the miniature paintings executed during Akbar's reign, Babur and Humayun are represented usually wearing *choga*s, coats, caps and cloaks. It appears that these costumes were in fashion during Akbar's reign. And when Akbar commissioned paintings of Babur and Humayun, they were depicted in these costumes. Costumes worn by Babur and his son Humayun were largely influenced by the Turkish or Mongol style, which gradually acquired a more Indian look during the reign of their successor, Akbar. In one of the paintings, in fact, Akbar has been shown wearing a *dhoti*.

(Sen, 1984, 9)

The social and cultural history of Akbar's reign is best documented in *Ain-i-Akbari*

An ageing Aurangzeb in a white jama*, turban and a bejewelled turban-band. c. 1700, British Library, Oriental and India Office Collections.*

Facing page:
Sultan Said Khan pays homage to Babur near Farghana. The costumes are notable in their drape and style. Baburnama, dated 1597/98, National Museum, New Delhi.

A farji *or coat-type jacket from Northern India.*

Above: *Detail. 20th century, National Museum, New Delhi.*

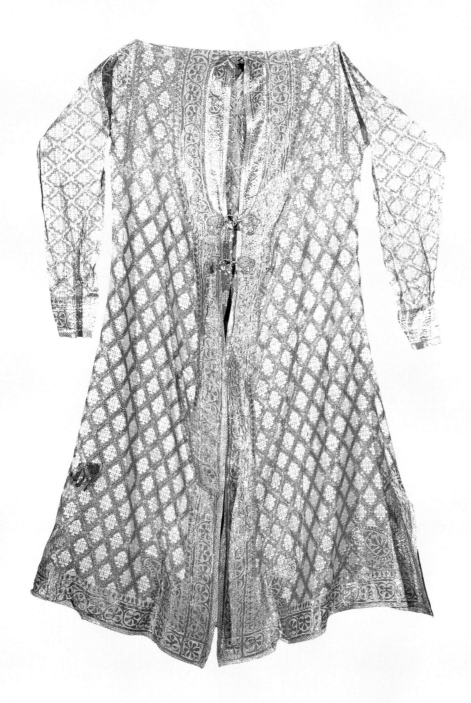

A jamdani choga *from Northern India.*

Above: *Detail. Late 19th century, National Museum, New Delhi.*

by Abu'l Fazl Allami and in a significant number of miniature paintings that have survived from his times, and that now form an important component of different art collections. Chapter 31 of *Ain-i-Akbari* mentions 'the wardrobe and the store for mattresses,' with details of the materials used for garments, the types and shapes of garments, and, more interestingly, Akbar's interest in coining Hindi words for common garments:

Instead of *jama* (coat), he says *sarbgati*, that is, covering the whole body; for *izar* (drawers), he says *yar-pirahan* (the companion of the coat); for *nimtana* (jacket), *tanzeb*; for *fauta*, *patgat*; for *burqa* (a veil), *chitragupita*; for *patka* (loincloth), *katzeb*; for *shal* (shawl), *parmnarm*; *takauchiya* (a coat without lining of Indian style); and similarly for the other names.

For the *takauchiya* Abu'l Fazl says:

Formerly it had slits in the skirt and was tied on the left side; his Majesty has ordered it to be made with a round skirt and to be tied on the right side.

Ain-i-Akbari, Abu'l Fazl Allami
(Translated by H. Blochmann, 96)

Paintings of this period prominently depict fastening the costumes differently. The Hindus fastened the outer garment towards the left armpit with tie-cords, while the Muslims fastened the tie-cords towards the right armpit.

Other literary works of Akbar's reign, such as the Persian translations of the epics Mahabharata and Ramayana, and some paintings depict Hindu gods in *dhoti*s, the indigenous attire. (Daljeet, 1999, 33) Another variation noticeable in paintings from Akbar's reign is the long *jama*, as seen in Mian Tansen's portrait in the National Museum, New Delhi. The great singer Tansen, one of the nine gems of Akbar's court, did not wear the usual courtly attire. In one of his portraits he wears a full-sleeved, white, long *jama* that almost touches his feet. The *Akbari*-style *patka*, turban and *angavastram* are also part of the attire. The *angavastram* is taken from under the right armpit over the left shoulder, its one end falling in front, while the other end is draped at the back. Tansen might have brought this attire from the court of Raja Ramchandra of Rewa, from where he had moved to the Mughal court. (Daljeet, 1999, 29)

While fashions change according to an emperor's tastes, it is not always possible to provide exact dates on the introduction of new costumes. Such information is rare to come by. One such reference pertains to a dress described by Jahangir in his memoirs *Tuzuk-i-Jahangiri*:

> Having adopted for myself certain special cloths and cloth stuffs, I gave an order that no one should wear the same but he on whom I might bestow them. One was a *Nadiri* coat that they wear over a *qaba* (a kind of outer vest). Its length is from the waist down to below the thighs, and it has no sleeves. It is fastened in front with buttons, and the people of Persia call it *Kurdi* (from the country of Kurds). I gave it the name of *Nadiri*.
> *Tuzuk-i-Jahangiri* (Translated by A. Rogers and H. Beveridge [Indian reprint], New Delhi, 1968, 384)

Portrait paintings of the Mughal emperors are an important source of information on costumes. In fact, emperors were often identified by their costumes and wearing styles. Paintings from Akbar's reign (found in the *Hamzanama*, *Tutinama* and *Akbarnama*) depict the *jama*, full-sleeved and short in length, falling slightly above the knees, and with four pointed ends (popularly known as *chakdar jama*). Usually the *jama* was worn with loose trousers and a turban or *atpati* in a particular style during

A kundan necklace shimmering with white topazes. 19th century, National Museum, New Delhi.

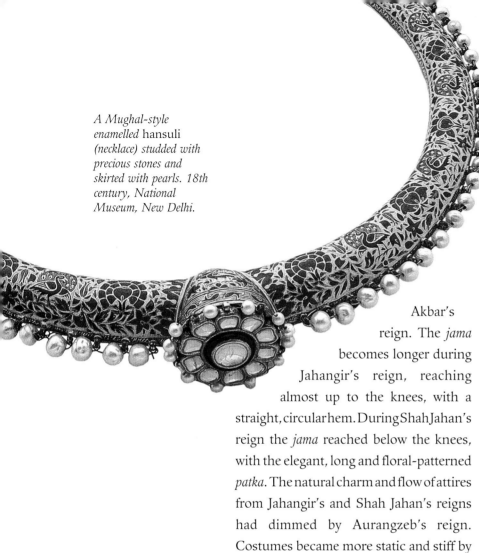

A Mughal-style enamelled hansuli (necklace) studded with precious stones and skirted with pearls. 18th century, National Museum, New Delhi.

Akbar's reign. The *jama* becomes longer during Jahangir's reign, reaching almost up to the knees, with a straight, circular hem. During Shah Jahan's reign the *jama* reached below the knees, with the elegant, long and floral-patterned *patka*. The natural charm and flow of attires from Jahangir's and Shah Jahan's reigns had dimmed by Aurangzeb's reign. Costumes became more static and stiff by then. By the 18th century, the time of the later Mughals and provincial courts, the *jama* reached up to the ankles.

The costumes of the common man find mention in accounts of foreign travellers. One such traveller was Chaplan Terry, who travelled in North India during Jahangir's reign. In his accounts, he mentions the dresses of the people in the countryside:

The habits both of the men and the women are little different, made for the most part of white cotton cloth. For the fashion, they are close, straight to the middle, hanging loose downward below the knees. They wear long breeches underneath, made close to their bodies, that reach to their ankles, ruffling like boots on the small of their legs. Their feet are bare in their shoes, which most commonly they wear like slippers... The men's heads are covered with long, thin wreathes of cloth, white or coloured, which go many times about them; they call it *sash*. They uncover not their heads when they show reverence to their superiors.

(Foster, 1921, 308)

Duarte Barbosa, the Portuguese writer and trader, gives interesting details about Indian costumes of the early 16th century. Barbosa describes the costumes of the Gujarati *bania* (trader) thus:

…They are clad in long cotton and silken shirts and are shod with pointed shoes of richly wrought cordivain: some of them wear short coats of silk and brocade…

(Dames, 1918, 113)

For the costumes of the women of Gujarat, Barbosa observes:

> Their dress is as long as that of their husbands; they wear silken bodices with tight sleeves, cut low at the back, and other long garments called *chandes* or *chaddar* that they throw over themselves like cloaks, when they go out, and on their heads they wear nought but their own hair well dressed on the top of it…
>
> (Dames, 1918, 113-114)

The Soldiers at Cambay wore coats of mail and jackets quilted with cotton.

(Dames, 1918, 119)

Of the Muslims, Barbosa says:

> They go very well attired in rich cloth of gold, silk, cotton and camlets (mixed silk and wool); they all wear turbans on their heads; those turbans are long, like Moorish shirts; drawers with boots up to the knees in very thick cordovan leather, worked in very dainty devices within and without the tip of the shoe.

(Dames, 1918, 119)

Shah Jahan's son Aurangzeb was not as inclined towards art as his ancestors. Therefore, the surviving paintings and works of his reign mark a continuity of the Shah Jahani style, but in a more static way. The usual attire of the Mughal courtier was the full-sleeved, long *jama* covering one-third the leg, with a circular

A woven silken shaluka *(full-sleeved upper garment for female) from Western India. Early 20th century, National Museum, New Delhi.*

hemline; the half-sleeved, front-open shirt over a golden-coloured garment, a long hanging *patka*, the *paijama* and a turban with a turban band. The over garment is short, up to the knees, with a fur collar. This kind of attire, with half sleeves and side slits, was found in paintings from Shah Jahan's reign. The *zari* or brocade dress had gained in popularity by this time.

After Aurangzeb, the Mughal Empire went into a steady decline. Regional centres grew as centres of power. The later Mughal rulers were not interested in art since they were busy safeguarding the throne. As a result, nothing new happened in the realm of art and culture. The few miniature paintings found of the later Mughal rulers seem to show that they just followed their ancestors' vestimentary style. During Emperor Akbar Shah II's reign (r. 1806-37), some paintings were executed by his court painters. In one such painting, the emperor and his courtiers have been shown wearing long *chogas/angarkhas/jamas*, loose *paijamas*, and turbans. The upper garment appears to be made of heavy material like *pashmina*, or *zari*-brocaded or *zari*-embroidered silk, and the lower garments are probably made of *mashru*. Some of them are wearing shawls as *kamarbands*. (Desai, 1985-86, 22)

Royal *karkhanas* were established

MOGUL.

MUNSHI.

ARAB JEMADAR.

ARAB HORSE DEALER.

SIKH.

BYRAGHY.

PHQRUD.

PARSEE BOY.

PARSEE GIRL.

during Akbar's reign, and costume manufacturing constituted one of the major units. Especially on the emperor's birthday, the *khilat* tailored in the fashion of the emperor's costume was offered to courtiers according to their ranks, and courtiers were obliged to wear the *khilat* to the court thereafter.

Gold jewellery—necklaces and *bajuband*s (armlets), to *sarpech*s (head ornaments) and girdles studded with gems—held great sway over all Mughal rulers. A number of paintings illustrate the Mughals' love for jewellery. One such portrait is of Shah Jahan as a prince holding a gold aigrette. (Strong, 1990, 79, 81, 82)

On birthdays Mughal rulers weighed themselves against coins, gems and fine clothing, which were later distributed among the poor. Such incidents have been mentioned by the European traveller Thomas Roe in his memoirs. (Roe, 1967, 214)

Shoes and slippers with *zardozi* embroidery were also used by the Mughals. And as depicted in paintings of the later Mughal period, shoes became more ornate with shoe tips curved up and inward rather flamboyantly. On the whole, the Mughal period was considered to be the most important and interesting phase in the history of Indian costumes.

Portrait of Zeenat Mahal. 19th century, National Museum, New Delhi.

THE VIJAYANAGARA EMPIRE (14TH-17TH CENTURIES)

~

The Vijayanagara Empire was founded in the 14th century, and became the dominant power in the Southern peninsula. The Vijayanagara style of architecture, sculpture and painting was a continuation of the Chola and Pandyan traditions. One of the greatest rulers of this dynasty was Krishnadevaraya, who was also a great warrior, scholar, painter and patron of fine arts. The *mandapa* (pillared porch) in the temples of Virabhadra at Lepakshi, Varadaraja at

Kanchipuram, Vithala at Hampi, and Jalakanthesvara at Vellore bear testimony to his patronage. The Vijayanagara Empire perhaps represents the last great phase of Indian history and culture.

The paintings at Lepakshi and the stone and bronze sculptures of the Vijayanagara period depict God with a crown, lots of jewellery, and a very ornamental lower garment and sash. On the ceiling of the Virupaksha Temple at Hampi, paintings depict Sage Vidyaranya's procession, where palanquin bearers and standard holders are wearing a tunic, a short *dhoti*, a *kamarband* and a turban. (Sage Vidyaranya was the great spiritual master responsible for the building of the Vijayanagara Empire in its earliest phase.) Women have been depicted wearing a sari, pleated in front, the end-piece taken under the right armpit and over the left shoulder, and then draped in front. They wear the usual ornaments—necklaces, earrings, bangles and rings, and have prominently depicted hair-buns. (Sivaramamurti, 1968, 117)

THE POST-MUGHALS (18TH-19TH CENTURIES)

~

After the Mughal rulers, provincial courts became powerful and some declared themselves independent. Some of the famous provincial courts were Avadh, Murshidabad and Punjab, while there were many others in the Rajputana region. During this period an attempt was made to capture the local identity of each provincial court in various ways, especially in the paintings of the era.

The Avadh provincial court evolved a self-conscious style. The cuts, falls/drapes and appearance of the garment vary from that of the Mughal court. Costumes like the *choga*, *angarkha*, *jama*, *paijama*, *ghagra*, *choli*, *farshi paijama*, *odhani* and sari of the later Mughal period worn by royalty and nobility, are housed in important museums and collections across the world: the City Palace, Jaipur; the Mehrangarh Fort, Jodhpur; the Victoria and Albert Museum,

Portrait of Bahadurshah Zafar. 19th century, National Museum, New Delhi.

London; the Mumtaj Mahal Museum and National Museum, Delhi; the Salarjang Museum, Hyderabad; and the Bharat Kala Bhawan, Varanasi, to name just a few.

By the early 18th century, during the reigns of Farrukhsiyar (r. 1713-19) and Muhammad Shah (r. 1719-48), the *jama* and the *angarkha*, which had already increased in length in the 17th century, came right down to the feet. An almost similar style was prevalent in the Avadh court. The *jama* became long and trailing, almost touching the feet. It was also high-waisted with lots of gathers. Full-sleeved *chapkan*, usually in *jamdani* work, with a short neck and a tight-fitted waist with little flare below, was also popular in the Avadh court. The *paijama* became wider, and was worn by men and women.

The *jama*, *choga*, *angarkha*, tight *paijama*, turban and *chaddar*/shawl were used more by men in the Punjab court in the 18th and 19th centuries. The *churidar paijama*, short *kurta*, *jama* and *odhani* were used by women during this period. The *baghalbandi*, *mirjai* and *sadri* were the other popular upper garments used by men in North India. The *kurta* was a new addition. It was a modified version of the old *nima* or *nimcha*. The focus was on elegant embroidery, patterning and the judicious

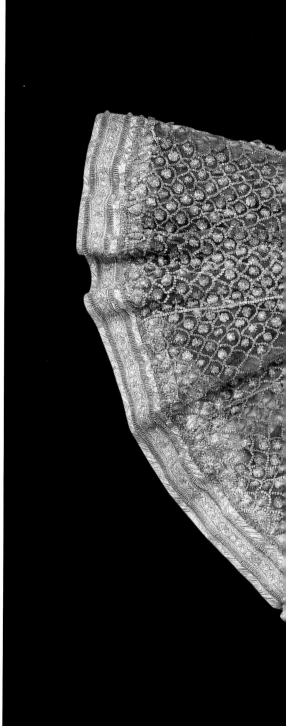

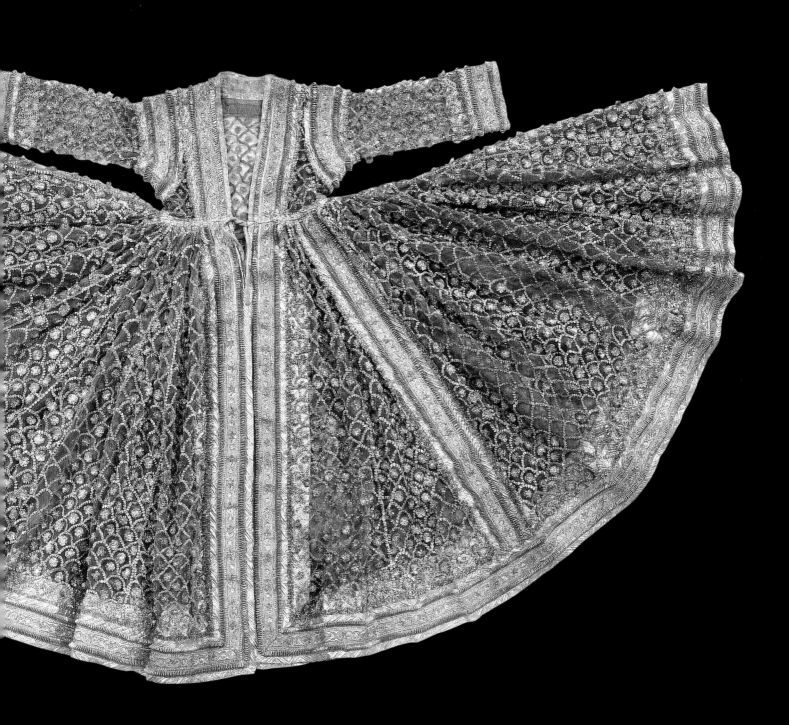

An elaborate Sikh turban. 19th century, Victoria and Albert Museum, London.

Intricately embroidered Parsi caps. 19th century, Victoria and Albert Museum, London.

selection of the material. Likewise, the *topi* and the *dupalli* were simply made of very light material, but elegantly finished and sometimes worn at a rakish angle.

The *angarkha*, as an outer garment, continued to be popular in the Rajasthan courts even in the 19th century. The *angarkha* yielded in part to a *chapkan*, a modification of a *balabar*, and became very popular among officials and servants in the circles connected with the officers of the court or the East India Company. In the late 18th and early 19th centuries, before the coat became popular, the *achkan*

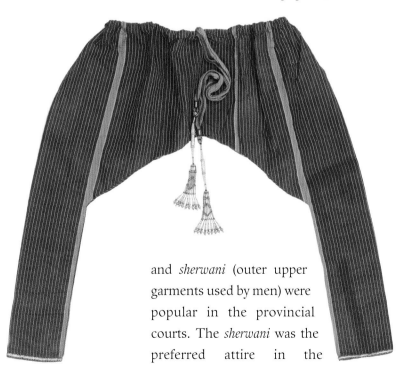

and *sherwani* (outer upper garments used by men) were popular in the provincial courts. The *sherwani* was the preferred attire in the

Hyderabadi court, while the *achkan* remained the choice of the Avadh court.

Under European influence, the *sherwani* and the *achkan* were used as upper garments by men. These tight-fitting costumes of varying length had a front opening with buttons, Chinese collars, drooping shoulders, full sleeves with cuffs, and two side pockets. The *paijama*, loose- (popularly known as *aligari*) or tight-fitting (*churidar*), were commonly used by men and women. During this period, apart from the *farshi paijama*, women of North India wore heavily embroidered *odhani*s, *ghagra*s and *choli*s. All these costumes were heavily brocaded, *zari*-embroidered, or tinsel-printed. A variety of dress materials was imported and soon became popular among the elite groups.

Today, while people residing in urban areas wear trousers, shirts, T-shirts, jeans and other Western wear, on special occasions they still prefer to wear the *sherwani*, *churidar paijama*, or *kurta paijama*. The *salwar*, *kameez* and *odhani*; the sari, blouse and petticoat; and the *ghagra*, *choli* and *odhani* are the traditional dresses of Indian women. In rural areas men still wear the *dhoti*, *kurta*, or long *kameez* and turban, while women continue to wear the traditional attire.

CONCLUSION

~

While it may be impossible to analyse the costumes of India through all historical time-frames and geographical expanses, within the scope of this book an attempt has been made to understand the development of Indian costumes for men and women in general, and in some elite groups, on the basis of extant literature and art.

Today, although a number of stitched attires are used by most Indians, outfits from drapes continue to be worn by men and women. Indeed, from drapes to stitched garments, Indian costumes have come a very long way.

A woollen achkan *from Northern India. 20th century, National Museum, New Delhi.*

Northern India

Present-day Jammu and Kashmir including Ladakh, Himachal Pradesh, Punjab, Haryana, Rajasthan, Uttar Pradesh, Delhi and the union territory of Chandigarh form the Northern region of India. Geographically this region is one of diversities, from snow-covered Himalayan ranges to plains and even a desert in Rajasthan. This area experiences a range of seasons—from a hot, dry summer to a humid, rainy season, to extreme cold with freezing temperatures at times. Apart from seasonal and geographical diversity, this region boasts of a unique cultural diversity as well. Since the very beginning of Indian history, people from different parts of the world have sought to gain access to India through this region for a host of reasons—political power, economic gains, religious activities, or travel. Many of them returned after fulfilling their desires, while some settled down here. The prominent ones were the Aryans, Greeks, Romans, Persians and Central Asians. They came to India with their own religious and cultural baggage, and left their mark on the cultural history of India.

Today, besides Hinduism, Buddhism, Sikhism and Islam, different local and folk traditions lend variety to the religious and cultural mosaic of Northern India. Within the ambit of this book, only the traditional costumes of this region have been touched upon.

The Northern region has a rich textile tradition, with each state being renowned for its own specialities. The entire Himalayan region is known for its tastefully and aesthetically created

Facing page:
A rich brocade choga *worn by warriors in Rajasthan. 19th century, National Museum, New Delhi.*

pashmina and *tus* shawls, as well as woollen fabrics. These colourful and intricately woven and embroidered shawls captured a sizeable chunk of the domestic as well as foreign markets around the late 18th-early 19th centuries. The *phulkari*s of Punjab and Haryana may not have been as successful as the *pashmina* shawls, but the former are evocative of a unique emotional association between the mother and the child. These *khaddar* (cotton) head coverings were made by a mother or grandmother soon after the birth of a child or grandchild. Replete with geometric patterns embroidered in colourful silken threads, these *phulkari*s were gifted to a daughter or daughter-in-law at the time of her marriage.

Rajasthan is well known for its costumes and textiles embellished with *bandhej* (tie-dye). This ancient art is famous for its use of bright colours. The earliest literary reference to *bandhej* is found in the *Harshacharita* dating back to the 6th century AD. The visual evidence of *bandhej* appeared in Cave no. 1 of Ajanta Caves (Aurangabad, Maharashtra), dating back to the late 1st century and early 2nd century AD. Cotton fabric, block-printed or *bandhej*-embellished, was used either for making garments or as a drape. While

Rajasthan is known for its splash of bright colours, Uttar Pradesh has made an invaluable contribution to Indian costumes – a unique use of white on white, popularly known as *chikan* work. The beauty of *chikan* work is highlighted by the fine intricate embroidery with white cotton thread on white cotton fabric. Patronised by the nawabs of Avadh (*c.* AD 1722-1856), *chikan* work was done mainly on *angarkha*s, *chapkan*s, *jama*s, *topi*s and *chaddar*s. During this period Delhi became one of the centres for *zari* embroidery on velvet, known as *zardozi* work. Apart from *zardozi* embroidery on furnishings (tents, canopies, palanquin covers, caparisons), *zari* embroidery is done on various kinds of garments ranging from saris, *odhani*s, *ghagra*s and *angarkha*s, to *patka*s and turbans. Caste and religion notwithstanding, from the shawl to the head covering, the *kurta* to the *ghagra*, each textile and costume has some kind of embellishment that may vary according to the region. The *chunari* (multicoloured tie-dyed), for instance, is mostly used in Rajasthani marriages, whereas the *odhani* with *gota kinnari* (*zari* threads of varying size worked into different patterns and designs) is used in weddings in Punjab, Haryana and Delhi. A colourful woollen

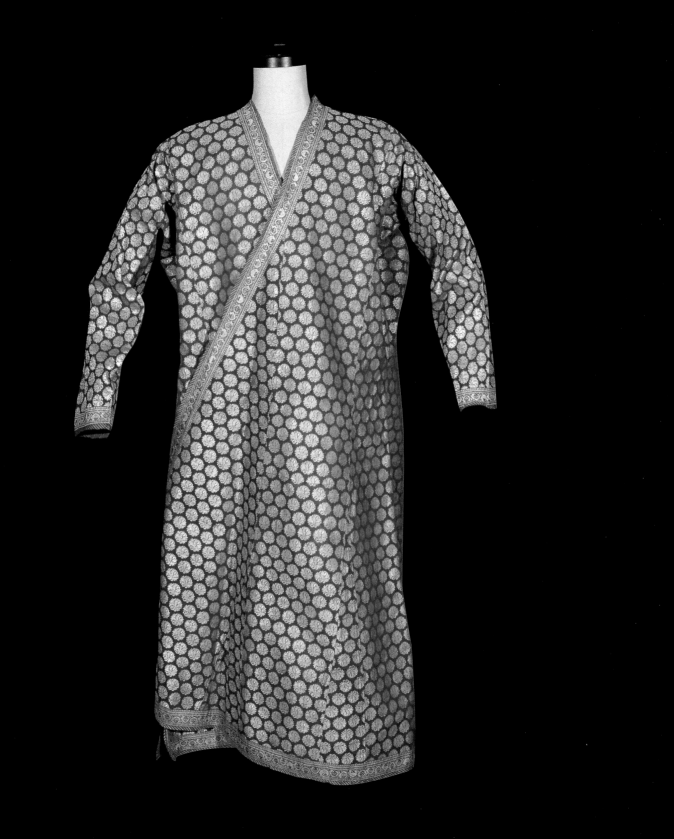

chaddar is used in the Himalayan region, while a *chikan*-embroidered *chaddar* is popular in Uttar Pradesh.

The Kashmiri outfit is markedly influenced by the Central Asian dress – loose robe and trousers, and the Turkmen cap. This style is evident even in terracotta sculptures found in the Ushkur, Akhur and Harwan regions. The Kashmiri dress for man and woman comprises a long, loose cotton or woollen *phiran* or smock, buttoned at the back and falling to the ankles. Usually, loose *paijama*s are worn under the smock. Women wear a crocheted skullcap called *karaba* by the Muslims and *taranga* by the Hindus. The fillet is red in the case of Muslim women, and white in the case of Pandit women. A shawl or white *chaddar* thrown gracefully over the head and shoulders completes their headgear. Men wear turbans as a sign of respectability and affluence. The ordinary peasant is content with wearing the long, pointed skullcap.

Jewellery like necklaces, armlets, waistlets, bracelets and earrings, and a special type of armlet called *Valaya kalapi* and earrings called *Kanaka nadi* are used by Kashmiris. Kashmiri jewellery is made of gold or silver with intricate designs. (Bamzai, 1973, 236-38)

Men in Himachal usually wear a *kurta*/shirt/*jama*, a *paijama*, and a *topi* with a woollen *chaddar*. In the entire Northern region, the *kurta*, shirt, or *jama* is the usual attire used for covering the upper part of the body. The *paijama* is usually *churidar*, either woollen or cotton for daily use, and with *zari* or brocade on silk for special

A cotton printed angarkha *from Rajasthan. 19th century, National Museum, New Delhi.*

Facing page:
A brocade choga *from Northern India. 19th century, National Museum, New Delhi.*

A woollen choga *from Northern India. 19th century, National Museum, New Delhi.*

A zari choga from Northern India. 19th century, National Museum, New Delhi.

occasions. The typical Himachal *topi* is a circular cap with a colourful flap raised in front. Women usually wear the *ghagra*, *peshwaz*, *choli* and *odhani*. The *peshwaz*, a woman's garment, is similar to the *jama* and the *angarkha*. It is made of fine material and has a high filled-out *choli*. Forbes Watson, a 19th-century author, says that the *peshwaz* was a favourite with Muslim brides.

The people of Punjab, Haryana, Rajasthan, Uttar Pradesh and Delhi largely prefer Muslim costumes, as these were the costumes of the rulers of this region from the 12th century onwards. People living in this region always adopted the costumes of their rulers. In fact, this practice was prescribed for official and ceremonial occasions, though at home they preferred wearing the traditional indigenous attire. At times people preferred the official dress, which then became as fashionable as the traditional dress.

The traditional dress of the men of Punjab and Haryana consists of a long shirt/*kurta*, a *paijama* and a turban. The *kurta* is a kind of tunic with sleeves, used to cover the upper part of the body. On ceremonial occasions men use an *achkan* over the shirt/*kurta*. The most common lower garment is the *paijama*, baggy and slightly gathered at the ankles. Apart from the *paijama*, men in Punjab wear the *tahmad*, which is like a *lungi*. Men in Haryana wear the *dhoti*. Some wear the *tahmad*. From the left, one end of the garment is taken around the waist to the right, drawn behind and simply tucked in at the back. The other end is gathered into a few pleats and tucked in at the navel without any further elaboration. The *dhoti* is worn in a traditional way. On the head men wear a conical cap or *kulah*, around which is folded a piece of cloth, with one end called the *sapha* flapping down behind the neck; or they simply put on a loosely folded turban called *pag*.

An elaborately embroidered cotton choli *from Himachal Pradesh. 19th century, National Museum, New Delhi.*

Facing page:
A kurta, choli *and an* odhani *set from Northern India. 19th century, Victoria and Albert Museum, London.*

Khilat: *The Robe of Honour*

~

Presenting the *khilat* or robe of honour to everyone present in the court was one of the important customs practised by the Mughals. Although this tradition was introduced in India by some of the Muslim rulers before the coming of the Mughals, the latter popularised this custom and made it into an elaborate affair.

During coronation anniversaries, the two Ids, birthdays of princes, or on any other special occasion, the emperor used to distribute *khilat*s. However, the status of the receiver was decisive in the number of garments he received. Those higher in status and importance received a higher number of garments. There were four to five degrees of the *khilat*, ranging from a three-piece set of garments to a seven-piece set. The regular category of the *khilat* was basically the three-piece set. These three garments were common to all categories, but the number of garments and other ornaments increased thereafter for each successive category. The first category, the three-piece set, consisted of a *jama* (long coat with full skirt), a *dastar* (turban), and a *kamarband* (waistband). The next category was of a five-piece set: a *balaband* (turban band) and a *sarpech* (turban ornament) were added to the first category. The third category had an additional *nimah astin* (tight-fitting jacket with short or half sleeves).

The seven-piece *khilat* consisted of a cap or a royal robe. This royal or grand robe was a coat with sleeves, like the *qaba* (full-sleeved garment used as outer wear), but with buttons instead of strings at the neck, chest and waist. Sometimes two pairs of drawers, two shirts and two girdles with a scarf also became part of this category of the *khilat*.

Receiving a *khilat* was considered a special mark of favour by the emperor, and the receiver had to actually wear it in the court. As a matter of rule, *khilat*s were also bestowed on important people when they presented themselves in the court, or took their leave of the emperor, or were appointed to important posts.

Facing page: A zari-embroidered choga *from Kashmir, 19th century; a zari and silk brocaded* sadri *and a zari brocaded* churidar *from Uttar Pradesh, 20th century. National Museum, New Delhi.*

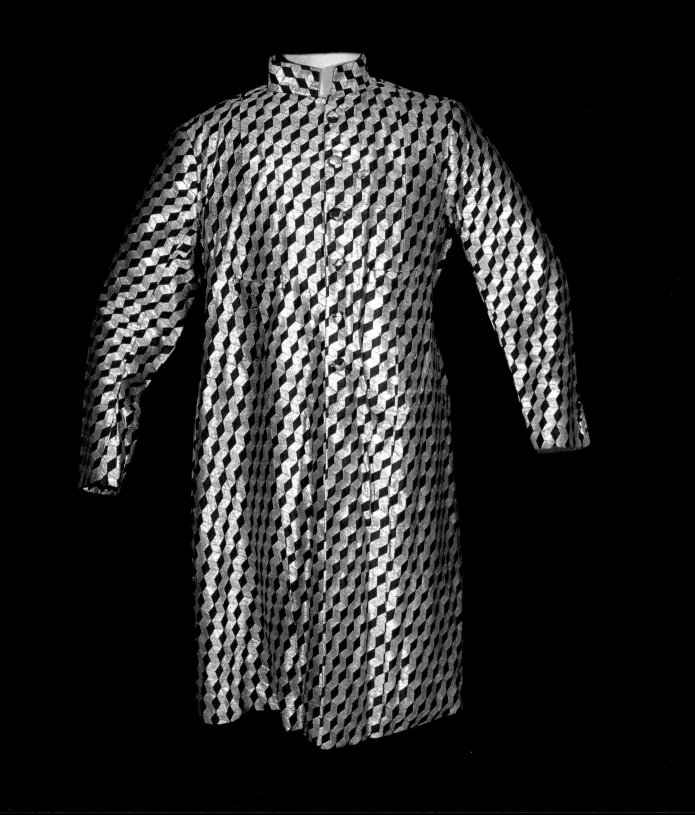

Women in Punjab and Haryana usually wear the *salwar*, *kameez* and *odhani*, or the *ghagra*, *kameez* and *odhani*. The *salwar* is a kind of *paijama*, almost like a man's *paijama*—except that a woman's *salwar* has a little more flare. The material used for a *salwar* is finer than the material used for a man's *paijama*. The *kameez* is an upper garment used by the women of Punjab and Haryana. This garment is different from both a man's *kurta* and the European shirt. In length it resembles a man's *kurta*, reaching up to the mid-thighs, but it is shaped to perfectly fit the figure and is not worn loose. Its length or sleeves, however, may vary according to the liking of a person or fashion trends. Hence, the *kameez* could be long or short, and full-, half- or three-fourth sleeved, or sleeveless. Typically, the women of Punjab and Haryana use a *chunni* or *dupatta* to cover their head. This is worn around the neck in such a manner that each of both ends fall either in front or at the back. Today, this Punjabi suit has become very popular not only all over North India, but even in the South.

Rajasthani men usually wear a three-piece attire: *bandia-angarkha*, *dhoti* and *sapha*. The *bandia-angarkha* is a closely fitted short coat, fastened with tie-cords either on the chest or to the left. Its sleeves are long and narrow. The *dhoti* or loincloth covers the lower part of the body, reaching

A silk brocade farshi paijama *embroidered with* zari *thread, from Northern India. Early 20th century, National Museum, New Delhi.*

Facing page:
A silk brocade achkan *woven with gold and silver* zari *thread, from Uttar Pradesh. 20th century, National Museum, New Delhi.*

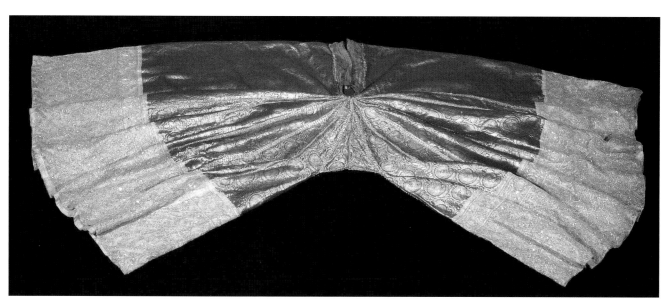

Facing page:
A silk and zari *kurta
with religious inscriptions
woven in, from Northern
India.*

practices of different communities. Women in Rajasthan wear the *ghagra* or *lehenga*, shirt and *odhani*. The Rajasthani *ghagra* has lot of gathers; sometimes close to twenty yards of cloth is used to make a single *ghagra*. A bodice called *kacali* is worn on the upper part of the body. The open-back, back-fastening bodice is either embroidered, tie-dyed, or block-printed. The *odhani* completes the attire. The usual style of wearing it is to take one end, tuck it in at the navel or the waist, and take the remaining portion across the left side to the back, from where it is taken over the head.

The act of decorating God with jewellery and colourful costumes in keeping with the festival and season, constitutes an important aspect of the Vallabhacharya Sampradaya's day-to-day activities in Rajasthan. The Vallabhacharya Sampradaya, founded by Vallabhacharya (*c.* 1472-1530), is one of the most significant Vaisnava sects in North India. Sri Nathji (Sri Krishna) is the chief icon of this sect and his youthful figure poised in the act of lifting Mount Govardhana is worshipped. The Lord's *mukhiya*s or attendants follow an elaborate routine put in place in His service. Sri Nathji is dressed differently

much below the knees. Male members of the royal family and important officials prefer to wear the *churidar paijama* instead of the *dhoti*, and a long *angarkha* or *achkan* instead of the *bandia-angarkha*.

Rajasthani *paga*s or *sapha*s are very colourful, and the wearing styles differ according to the status, occasions and

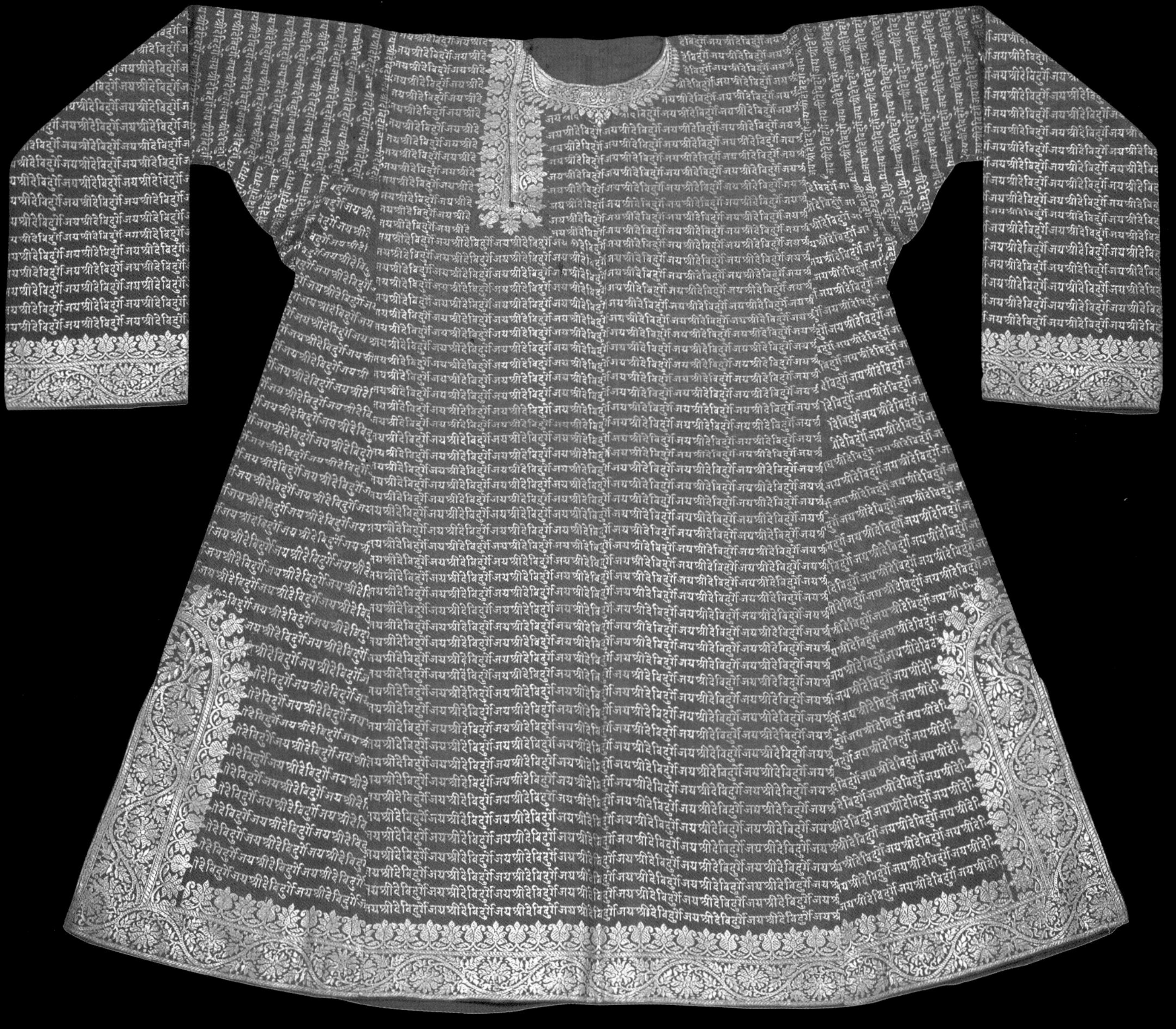
जय श्री देवि दुर्गे

A silk and zari achkan *from Northern India. 20th century, National Museum, New Delhi.*

A quilted brocade jama *from Rajasthan. 19th century, National Museum, New Delhi.*

A silk and zari paijama *from Northern India. 19th century, National Museum, New Delhi.*

Facing page:
The detail of a velvet choga *embroidered with* zari *thread, from Northern India. Early 20th century, National Museum, New Delhi.*

kurta/long shirt, turban and *angavastram*. On formal occasions they use *achkan/ kurta*, *paijama* and *turban*/cap. Women prefer the sari, blouse, petticoat and *chaddar*, or the *ghagra*, *choli* and *odhani* for everyday as well as formal wear. For everyday wear women prefer cotton, while *zari* or brocade on silk is preferred for special occasions.

The origin of one of the classical dance forms of India, Kathak, is attributed to Uttar Pradesh. Kathak originated from the simple devotional mime of the *Kathaka*s, originally a caste of story-tellers or balladeers (mainly episodes from the epics), attached to certain temples. Both men and women performed this dance, especially in the court of the nawabs of Avadh around the late 18th- early 19th centuries.

The costume and jewellery of the dancers are very colourful. The male dancer wears a light *paijama*, a flowing long coat, and a tunic or *peshwaz*, while the female dancer wears a tight-fitting *paijama* and a long and open, loose gossamer outfit with a *dupatta*. The dancers wear necklaces, bangles, *jhumar*s (head ornaments) and *bajuband*s (hand ornaments) as dominant pieces of jewellery.

for each *darsana* (view or apparition) to His devotees, and during the main festivals.

The costumes of the men and women of Uttar Pradesh are more or less similar to those of the entire Northern region. Men generally prefer *dhoti/lungi*,

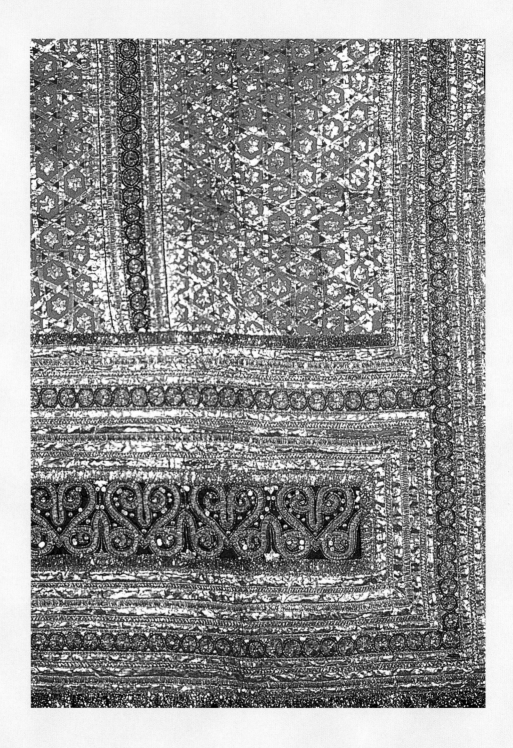

The detail of an odhani *embroidered with* zari *thread typical of Western and Northern India. 20th century, National Museum, New Delhi.*

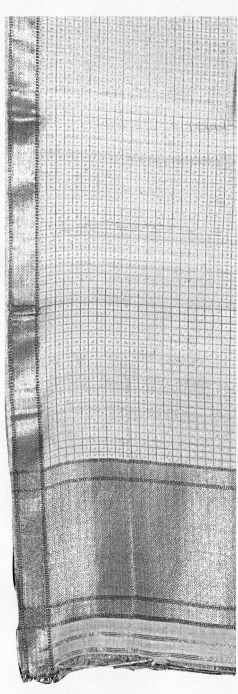

Left: A zari turban cloth from Rajasthan. 20th century, National Museum, New Delhi.

A silk odhani from Uttar Pradesh. 20th century, National Museum, New Delhi.

83

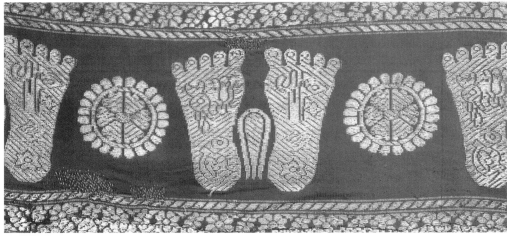

A silk and zari namavali *shawl from Uttar Pradesh. Below: Detail.* Namavali *shawls are either woven or printed over with religious inscriptions. 19th century, National Museum, New Delhi.*

Apart from classical dance forms, each state has a rich folk-dance tradition with an immense variety of costumes and accessories.

The sari, *ghagra*, *kameez*, *kurta*, long shirt, *achkan* and *jama* are the main traditional garments of men and women in the Northern region of India. It is understood that the folk dancers of Braj Pradesh (Vrindavan, Gokul and Mathura), the various ethnic groups in Rajasthan and the entire Himalayan region have variations in their dances, costumes and textiles. Religious groups too have distinct identities, corroborating once again that a myriad factors add to the rich tradition of textiles and costumes of India.

EASTERN AND NORTHEASTERN INDIA

Bihar, West Bengal, Orissa and Jharkhand comprise Eastern India. Adjacent to Eastern India is the Northeast, popularly known as the seven sisters – Arunachal Pradesh, Assam, Mizoram, Manipur, Nagaland, Meghalaya and Tripura. The entire Eastern and Northeastern India is very rich in natural resources. The people of this region are reputed to have a great love for art and culture. Topographically, parts of the Himalayas touch the region of Asom (Assam), Arunachal Pradesh and the upper part of Bengal. The Ganga River flows through Bihar and West Bengal, and merges into the Bay of Bengal. The Brahmaputra flows through Assam and Bangladesh, while the Mahanadi River passes through Orissa. Hence, Eastern and Northeastern India is rich in fertile plains as well. This region enjoys a moderate climate. The heaviest rain zone of India, Cherapunjee, is also situated in this region, in Meghalaya. The fertile land of the east favours the production of the world-famous *mulmul* (muslin), popularly known as *Dhakkai mulmul*. *Mulmul* is considered to be a wonder fabric, which can pass through a ring. Besides fine *mulmul* and cotton, this region is also known for its variety of silk production. The silk Baluchari saris of Murshidabad (West Bengal), *moga* silk *mekhala* of Assam (Northeast), and the silk *chaddar*s of Bhagalpur (Bihar) are very well known. Apart from silk drape wear, different varieties of colourful silk yardage are also produced, which are used to make costumes for men and women of this region.

Facing page:
A loose-fitting brocade paijama *from Eastern India. 19th century, National Museum, New Delhi.*

A silk baluchari *sari from West Bengal.*
Below: *Detail.*
19th century, National Museum, New Delhi.

The early archaeological remains, epigraphic evidences and travel accounts corroborate the existence of a rich textile tradition in the past. The tradition has been carried forward efficiently to the present times. Early terracotta sculptures (2nd century BC-3rd-4th centuries AD), especially the *yakshi* images of Chandraketugarh (North 24 Parganas, roughly 40 kilometres northwest of Kolkata), depict beautiful attires with elegant fall and flare. (Pal, 2002, 60) Finds from the archaeological sites corroborate remarkable urban growth during the reigns of the Sungas and the Kushans.

Excavation finds of bone and metal spindle whorls, terracotta spools, weavers' shuttles and metal needles from Mahananda (4th-5th centuries, Gupta period) and Pala period (9th-10th centuries) sites indicate that textile weaving was the popular cottage industry of these periods. Export of Bengal cotton can be traced back to the 1st-2nd centuries. Kautilya's *Arthashastra* (compiled and enriched between 3rd century BC and 3rd century AD) gives important information on textile trade within this region and the outside world. The text further refers to the term *Vanga*, which means 'fabric of Bengal.' Periplus and Ptolemy, Greek writers of the 1st-2nd centuries AD, refer to the great ports of Tamralipta (present Midnapore district) and the river Ganga, from where textiles of Bengal were exported to ancient Greece and Egypt. Tamil literature mentions the term *Kalinga*, which means 'cotton from Kalinga' (Orissa). Cotton fabrics of Kalinga were very popular during the 2nd-3rd centuries in the domestic market of Southern India. Even today, cotton-silk saris woven in *ikat* technique remains a speciality of Orissa. The superior quality of cotton and silk produced by the skilled artisans of this

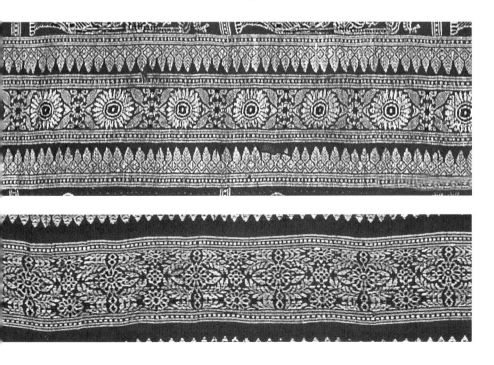

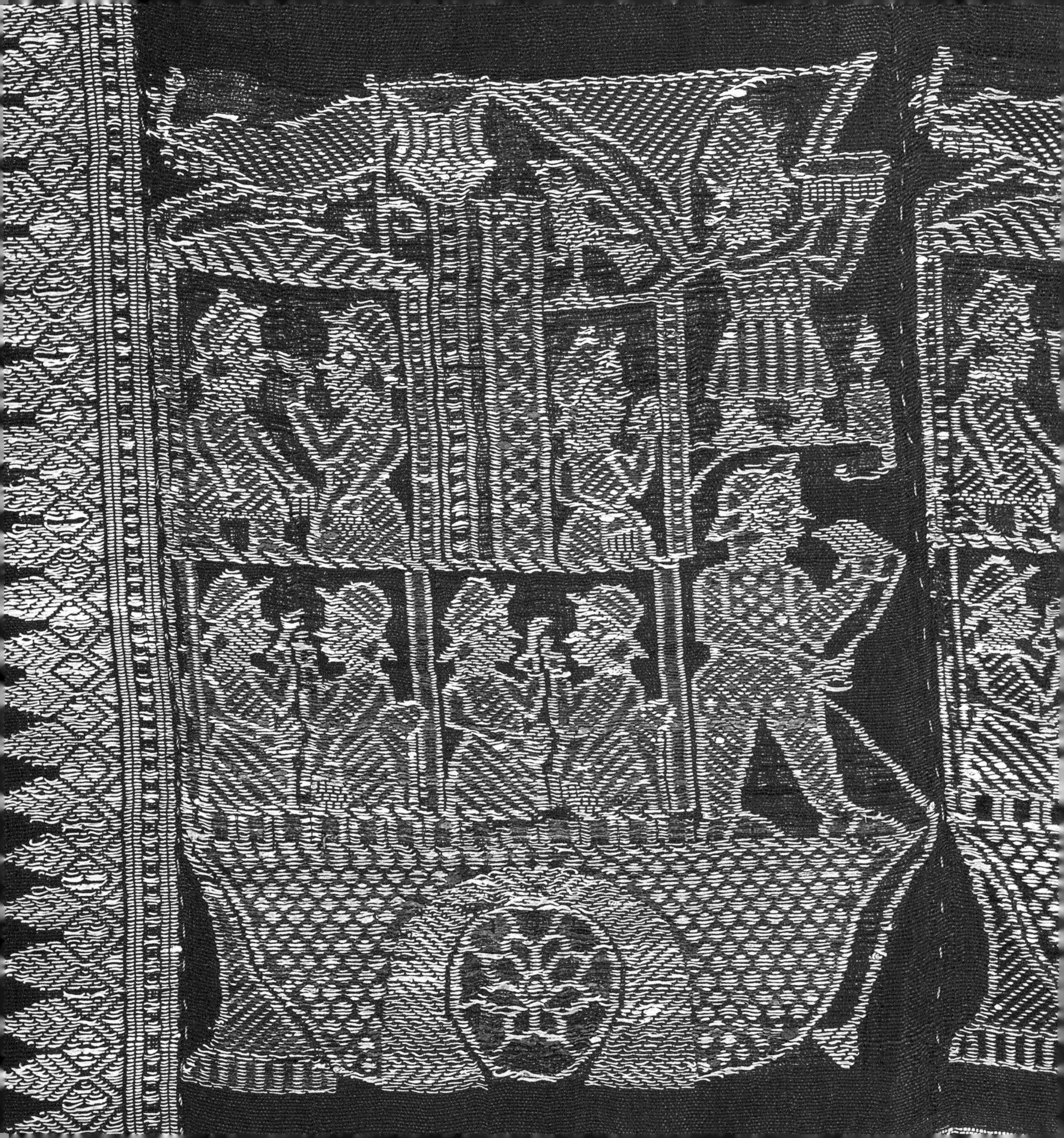

region has attracted traders from all over the world. Cotton *jamdani*s, *satgaon* quilts and *nakshi kantha*s were exported to different countries in the past. Traders visited India frequently and their tastes and demands influenced products made for the export market. The costumes of foreigners, however, did not influence the costumes used by the people of this region, who continued to wear their traditional unstitched attire. Muslim and British rules (13th-19th centuries) strongly influenced stitched garments, so the *choga*/*jama*/coat and *paijama*/trousers became the attire for men. The usual dress for women was the sari, petticoat and blouse, or the *lehenga*, *choli* and *odhani*. On the whole, both types of costumes, stitched and unstitched, were equally common among men and women depending on the occasion on which these were to be worn.

Bihar is known for its quality silk production. The silk *chaddar* or shawl (from Bhagalpur) is famous for its quality. Men in Bihar wear the *kurta* or *kameez* as the upper garment, and the *dhoti* or *paijama* as the lower garment. As everyday wear, a *chaddar* covering the upper part of the body is taken over the *kurta* and *dhoti*. Apart from the main dress, men take a *gamcha* over the shoulder. At times, the *gamcha* is also used as a *kamarbandh*. Traditionally women prefer the sari, blouse and petticoat. Cotton printed saris form part of everyday wear. Earlier, saris were worn in the *sidha palla* style, whereas today the *ulta palla* style of wearing the sari has become more popular among the urban elite. Silk shawls embellished with floral patterns on borders and end-pieces are used to cover the upper part of the body. On the whole, the costumes of Bihar are quite simple and elegant.

In Bengal, as is evident from stone and terracotta sculptures, paintings and coins, the men's traditional attire consists of two pieces: the *uttariya* or mantle cloth used to wrap around the upper part of the body, and the *adhovasta* used for covering the waist and the lower part of the body. The *dhoti* was the prime men's costume.

The *dhoti* is wrapped around the waist, gathered in front and passed between the legs, and then tucked behind. It is fastened securely to the waist with a *kamarband* or *pheta* tied in bow-shaped knot. The most fascinating part of men's *dhoti* is its pleats, which fall to the right. Sometimes, the *dhoti* has a beautiful, colourful narrow border, which falls in front when the pleats are made. *Patka*s or sashes adorn

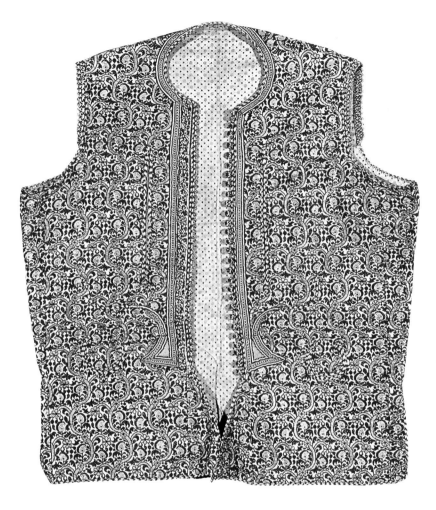

A woven himru sadri *from West Bengal. Late 19th century, National Museum, New Delhi.*

the waist over the men's upper garment. These *patka*s are embellished with fine floral patterns and tassels. Woollen *chaddar*s or shawls over *dhoti*s and *kurta*s are quite commonly worn by men of this region. These *pashmina* shawls have plain fields and narrow floral borders either woven or embroidered.

In the days of yore, the women of Bengal wore saris with *kamarband*s. The Bengali woman's sari-wearing style is different from other wearing styles prevalent in India. It is wrapped around the waist like a sarong, and the full width of the *pallu* (end-piece) falls in front. This style of wearing the sari is quite graceful and elegant. Saris of Bengal are made either of silk or cotton, known as *taat*. The *taat* sari usually has a plain field with small *buti*s and stripes on the end-piece and border. A blouse and, later, a petticoat completed the attire. Apart from *taat* saris, which are used more often for everyday wear, silk *baluchari* and *tangail* saris are worn by women of the elite group. These silk and *zari* saris are usually worn on special occasions as well. *Baluchari* saris are known for their elaborate *aanchal*s (end-pieces) and contrasting colour schemes (maroon, purple or red field patterned with off-white and yellow silk threads). Visually rich, these saris have heavy end-pieces, plain or small *butidar* fields, and floral borders. The end-piece is the most fascinating part of the sari, with large-sized *kalka buteh*s in the centre surrounded with decorative patterns arranged in blocks. There are a variety of patterns; a nawab smoking *huqqa*; a nawab holding flower; a mother and a child; a horse rider; an elephant rider; or a ship and a boat, among others. The finest woven cottons of Bengal are the *jamdani*s. The *jamdani* weavers of Dacca were extremely skilful and valuable. During Aurangzeb's reign (1658-1707), high annual tributes were paid by Dacca to the emperor, the major portion being generated from *jamdani* weaving. White with white is a special feature of this art— the base yarn is cotton and the pattern woven on it is also in white thread. Fine-quality *jamdani* was created in white or multicoloured thread, with floral or *butidar* patterns. Apart from saris, *jamdani* yardage made during this period was also used for making garments. The *jama* and the *angarkha* were the popular costumes made from it, especially for the elite of Bengal. Intricate as well as fine cotton and silk weaving constituted the art of weaving in Bengal.

Dye-resist *ikat* weave is the speciality of Orissa, while colourful, geometric-patterned weaves are typical of Jharkhand. Cotton appliqué, cotton and silk embroidery, *batik* and block printing are the other techniques used for decorating the textiles of this region. The traditional garments for men of this region are *kurta*,

dhoti and cap/turban. The *kurta* is a kind of shirt or tunic with long or half sleeves (it could be sleeveless as well), and buttoned up at the centre on the chest. Apart from the *kurta*, *chapkan* and *achkan*, the *angarkha* and the *jama* are other upper garments used by the men of this region on formal occasions. The common upper garment used by men is the *bagalbandi* or the short, close-fitting coat. It has a double

The detail of the woven himru sadri (facing page) highlights the intricate work of the weavers of 19th-century West Bengal.

Bride's Attire: Two Lakh Rupees

~

Shah Jahan and Mumtaz Mahal's favourite son Dara Shikoh (1615-59) was married to Nadira Begam. The wedding mentioned in the *Padshahnama*, is supposed to have taken place on the 2nd *Shaban* (eighth month of the Muslim calendar) of 1042 AH (Hijra era), or 12th February, AD 1633. Mumtaz Mahal was very eager to see her son married, but died before this could come to pass. Her eldest daughter Jahanara Begam left no stone unturned to ensure the marriage ceremonies were held as desired by her late mother.

The text *Padshahnama*, which gives a detailed account of Shah Jahan's reign, also gives an elaborate description of Dara Shikoh's wedding, considered to be the most expensive wedding of that period. Around thirty *lakh* rupees were spent on the wedding, and Jahanara alone contributed sixteen *lakh*. Jahanara sent the first gifts with the *sachaq*, the auspicious red costume for the bride, to her prospective sister-in-law, Nadira Begam. This exclusive attire cost close to two *lakh* rupees.

Dara Shikoh's wedding procession was marked by fanfare, gaiety and a majestic display of colourful costumes.

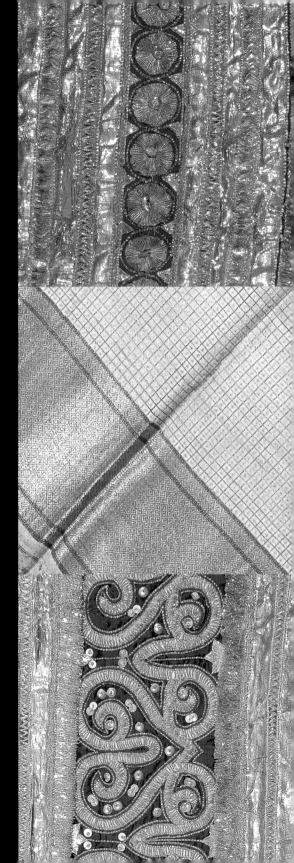

Weavers often wove grand themes, Indian and European, in the baluchari *saris of West Bengal. Below: Details. 19th century, National Museum, New Delhi.*

flap, the upper flap tied to the left with another flap under it. This full-sleeved attire is also known as the *mirjai*. The sleeveless variety known as *bandi* or *phatui*, is more used by men and women of a less privileged strata of society. The *dhoti* is worn in the fashion the men of Bengal and other regions wear it.

In the eastern part, the turban is simpler and seems to resemble types of

Some officials of Orissa and Bengal wear the *jama*, or a sort of tunic, and a *paijama*. A full-length long coat coming up to the knees with front opening and buttons, is worn over the tunic. A *chaddar* or shawl is generally wrapped over the coat by the common man by way of everyday wear, while the elite wear a loose overcoat-like attire.

Women of Orissa usually wear sari,

Rajasthani and Marathi turbans. Some people in the Northeast, West Bengal and Bihar use the *angavastra* or the *gamcha*, which serve the twin purpose of a turban and a scarf. *Angoocha* is a Prakrit form of the Sanskrit word *angavastra*, which means 'cloth for the body.' It appears further to be transformed into *gamcha*.

blouse and petticoat. They wear six-yard-long saris with bright borders. The sari is wrapped around the waist, the rest taken from the right side and over the left shoulder, leaving the right arm and shoulder quite free. The *saluka* or *sadri*, a half-sleeved tunic, is worn by the women of this region.

The women of the Northeast create costumes for their own use, and sometimes for the men also. Women weave sarongs and shawls on loin looms and frame looms. The usual practice is to weave the textile

in pieces and stitch these together later, to make the complete cloth. Woven jackets worn by the Mishimis, an ethnic group of the Northeast, are woven in two pieces that are then stitched together. The Lotha Nagar shawl is woven in nine parts and stitched together to make a single piece.

According to popular belief, the *muga* silk of Assam was introduced by the Bodo tribes, who had migrated from Central Asia. They brought the art of weaving and silk reeling with them. Traditionally, white or colourful cotton or silk *gamcha*s are woven with colourful broad borders in red silk thread. These are woven by the young woman of the house, and she gifts these to the eldest family member. The silk *mekhala* sarong is the traditional dress for the women of Assam. These are woven from gold-coloured *muga* silk. A fine *chaddar*, matching with a *muga* silk *mekhala*, is an essential part of a wedding and other ceremonial occasions.

There are special groups, too, who wear specific kinds of dresses. There are groups of dancers both folk and classical. Each ethnic group has its own dance costumes. For classical dances, however, the costumes follow a code. Of the six main schools of classical dance of India, two belong to this region: Odissi from the

East and Manipuri from the Northeast. According to popular belief, Odissi originated in the 2nd century BC during the reign of the Jain king Kharavela. In this dance form, the dancer wears an *ikat* silk sari of Orissa with beautifully contrasted colours. The dancer also wears heavy jewellery such as a wide waistband, elaborate hair ornaments, beautiful necklaces, bangles, *bajuband*s and anklets made of silver or gold.

Manipuri is also an early form of dance prevalent in Manipur. This dance is mainly devoted to Krishna and Radha, and the most popular dance is the *rasa* dance. Male dancers wear yellow *dhoti*s, *kamarband*s and head ornaments with peacock feathers. Female dancers wear a skirt bereft of pleats, which drapes stiffly. Over this skirt is worn a shorter, stiffer, thinner skirt resembling a ballet dancer's tutu. A colourful tight-fitting jacket accentuates the slim waistline, and a studded veil is draped from a decorative coiffure.

The East and the Northeast, thus, have a vast range of extremely elegant and colourful costumes. Traditionally, both stitched and unstitched costumes are worn by men and women in keeping with the occasion.

The rich textile tradition and cultural heritage of this region makes the East and the Northeast a prolific production centre of some of the best fabrics in India. Sculptures and paintings amply bear out the fact that the people of this region have always worn simple and graceful attire with elegant jewellery. Till today, they have not abandoned their vestimentary traditions.

WESTERN AND CENTRAL INDIA

Gujarat, Maharashtra, Madhya Pradesh, Goa, and the union territories of Dadra and Nagar Haveli, and Daman and Diu comprise Western and Central India. Geographically, this region has a long coastline along the Arabian Sea, the hills of the Vindhya region and the forest area of Vidharba (Maharashtra). The deep and dense forest region of Vidharba, which divides it from South India, was considered to be one of the most inaccessible parts of India by military strategists of the past. Climatically, the Western and Central regions do not have temperatures as freezing as those up North. The climate of these regions ranges from moderate, dry and cold to humid. Moreover, the sea, hills and forests make this region rich in natural resources. The easy sea- and land-route access helped the people of this region to develop close contact with the outside world. The finds of Harappan seals from Mesopotamia, Sumer and other ancient cultures provide clear evidence of trade relations between the people of this region and the outside world from ancient times. A large number of ethnic groups such as the Gurjars, Yanvans and Sakas came to India from Central Asia and Greece. Some like the Gurjars and Sakas settled in Western India. The resultant interaction and inter-mingling of the indigenous people and the foreigners largely account for the great cultural diversity of this area. While the Western and Central regions have absorbed many foreign influences, they have also retained much of the distinctive traditions of their own culture. The textiles and costumes of these regions constitute a

Facing page:
A brocade lehenga embroidered with gold thread at the border along the hemline, from Gujarat. 19th century, National Museum, New Delhi.

A Maratha silk turban embroidered with gota work, from Western India. 19th century, National Museum, New Delhi.

legacy that has drawn the best from both worlds.

Traces of the Harappan Civilisation (*c.* 2700-1750 BC) and the Chalcolithic culture (*c.* 1400-900 BC) are evident from various sites in Gujarat and Maharashtra. Most archaeologists are agreed upon Saurashtra being the earliest region for cotton production. Finds of spindles for spinning and twisting yarn, iron needles and awls for stitching, and terracotta pottery with impressions of woven fabric clearly indicate that weaving was widely practised in this region even in the Harappan period. (Lal, 1998, 14-15; Possehl, 1999, 249-50) Archaeologically, the earliest-known excavated printed cotton pieces (10th-11th centuries) have been found at Fustat near the Red Sea. These pieces, housed in museums in the United Kingdom, the United States of America, Germany and France, have been scientifically analysed and the reports indicate that these belong to Gujarat. (Guy, 1998, 186)

Rich Chalcolithic culture found at various sites in Maharashtra and the rock-cut architecture of Ajanta, Ellora, Elephanta, Karle and Bhaja, show early traces of civilisation in this region. The earliest evidence of actual silk thread from Nevasa (district Ahmednagar, Maharashtra) and linen fibre at Chandoli, (district Pune, Maharashtra), and iron and bone needles found from various sites indicate that textile weaving was prevalent in this region from very early times. (Saraswat, 2002-2003, 531) Finds of rock paintings and stone sculptures, along with literary evidence from Central India, either depict or refer to costumes made of different kinds of material (bast, cotton and silk). Goa was under Portuguese dominance from 1510 to 1961, and, therefore, Portuguese cultural influence is evident in the lifestyle of the local residents including in their costumes. Traditional textile weaving with cotton, silk and *zari* exists in each and every state. These garments are further embellished through a variety of techniques – print, embroidery, painted, tie-dyed and *bandhej*, among others.

People of Western and Central India wear stitched as well as unstitched garments. The men's traditional unstitched garments are *dhoti*, freshly folded turban, and *patka* or *kamarband*.

Besides, men also wear stitched costumes like tunic, *kurta* and *badiyan* as an upper garment. Similarly, women wear the sari as a traditional costume, apart from the *lehenga*. Locally produced yardages of different varieties are used for making different costumes.

The traditional costume for ordinary Gujarati men is a three-piece attire: *dhoti* or *paijama*, short jacket and *pagadhi/saphe* (turban). The *paijama* is less prevalent than the *dhoti*. The *dhoti* is tucked in at the back in the *kachcha* style.

The traditional lower garment for men of most classes is the *dhoti*, known as *dhotar* in Marathi. The *dhoti* has a narrow, coloured border. Men wear *dhoti*s in the following manner: it is first wrapped around the waist, then the rest of the *dhoti* is pleated breadth-wise from the right, and tucked in at the navel.

Over the *dhoti*, men in Western and Central India usually wear the *barabandi* or *barakasi* as an upper garment. It is a short coat/jacket known in the older tradition as *bandan*, *badiyan*, or *caubagala*, since it has four tie-cords. Usually it is fastened with six pairs of tie-cords. Each of the two flaps has three pairs of tie-cords. The upper flap is fastened to the left, and the narrow sleeves have horizontal folds

like bracelets. For formal occasions men use longer coat-like *jama*s or *angarkha*s, which they usually wear over the *barabandi*. A scarf or *dupatta* completes the attire. The *jama* is an outer garment, fitted snugly at the chest with a flaring skirt. Usually it is fastened under the right or left armpit with tie-cords.

The long full-sleeved *angarkha* is an outer garment, stitched in two parts: the upper and the lower. The upper part of the *angarkha* has an oval or V-shaped cut at the chest. It has a tie-cord in front, with an inner flap or *parda*, which covers the chest elegantly. The flaring lower portion of the *angarkha* may vary in length according to the period or the taste of the user.

Along with the *dhoti* and *jama*, men use turbans as part of their

A brocade paijama *from Central India.*
19th century, National Museum, New Delhi.

traditional attire. The turban has a social significance and is used in keeping with the economic status of a person. Men use pre-formed *pagadi*s or freshly folded turbans, also known as the *phete* or *sapha*. Plain cotton *phete*s are used for everyday wear, while brocaded turbans are used

higher and the entire turban is fitted to one side of the head, with the other squat side covering the ear. The 3- or 4-pointed high cap covers the forehead. Till date, the white *khaddar*, stitched Gandhi *topi* is very common among Marathi men. This small *topi* is worn vertically on the head.

In Gujarat and Maharashtra, the traditional outfit for women is the sari. The ensemble consists of three pieces – *sari*, *blouse* and *petticoat*. Gujarati women usually wear the *sidha palla* sari, similar to the North Indian rural women's wearing style. Maharashtrian women wear a full nine- or ten-yard-long sari, traditionally in the *kachcha* style—also known as the *langhavali dhoti* as it is taken between the legs. This style of wearing the sari was prevalent in ancient India.

Saris are made of different materials with different techniques, according to the needs and tastes of the different ethnic groups of the region. The most famous ones are the silk *patola* from Patan, satin silk *bandhej* from the Kutch region, silk and zari *ashawalli* from Ahmedabad, *tanchoi* from Surat, and *paithani* from Paithan. *Patola*s are known for the high-quality workmanship of the Patan weavers and dyers. Worked in subdued colours (dark maroon, pale green, indigo blue and ivory

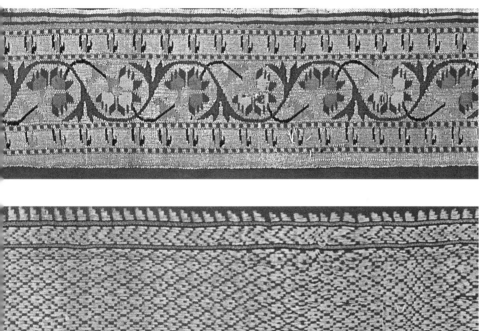

during weddings and other ceremonies. The turban is worn or tied differently by different ethnic groups in Gujarat. In the pre-formed turban, one side is slightly

Kapad Battisi: *Thirty-two Fabrics*

~

Written in the 17th century, *Kapada Chintani* and *Kapada Kutuhal* are two compositions that provide the names of fabrics and costumes prevalent during this period. Appended to these works is a list of fabrics popularly known as *kapad battisi*, which means 'thirty-two fabrics'.

This descriptive literature may not boast of high literary merit, but it is composed in the form of couplets or popular sayings. These couplets are composed in Hindi-oriented Brijbhasa, often very useful in educating the layman and frequently quoted in conversation

Kapada Chintani was composed by Madhodas from Pahuna village of Mewar state in Rajasthan, in Vikram Samrat 1730 (AD 1673). The *Chintani* consist of 31 couplets, with one incomplete couplet. This manuscript is in the Khas-Mohar collection in Maharaja Sawai Man Singh II Museum in Jaipur, Rajasthan.

Caste and religion notwithstanding, Indian textiles and costumes are known to be intricately embellished in techniques that differ from one state to another, including in manners that differ in pockets within each state.

Given below are the translations of some interesting couplets:

Radha, who is bursting with youth,
dresses herself up as Krishna wearing
a *Pitambar* (literally, yellow dress) at her waist, donning a
peacock crown on her head and
loudly playing the flute. (14)

The dearest one who is the life
of my life has gone to a distant place.
Without him there is no life left and
Masaru (semi-silk fabric) burns my body like fire. (15)

He has spent the night making love
with the other one (out of wedlock) and
here I am sitting with eyes
as red as *Kasumba* (linen, bast fibre). (21)

Kapada Kutuhal was composed by Prayagdas, who hailed from Udaipur, the capital of the former Mewar state. His couplets suggest the use of different types of fabrics, and he gave names of fabrics without using puns. This manuscript is not dated, but from the style and language of the text, it appears to have been written in the 17th century. Given below are the translations of some interesting couplets:

His *jama* (upper garment) is made of *zardozi* and he is wearing a *soothan* (*paijama*) of *Pat* (silk): thus attired the lord has come home, I could cling to his neck. (1)

Her *kanchuki* (blouse) is made of *neelak* (blue) and she is covered with a *chira* (*odhani* or a long wrapping cloth). Her *lehenga* (long skirt) of the *lungi* variety is looking very graceful on the lovely lady. (2)

Her sari is of *tansukh* (silk and cotton) fabric, with a fine-fitting *kanchuki*, and a jewel-studded *beharakha* (a padded arm-band) graces the lovely lady's body. (15)

The above-mentioned texts give the standard list of textiles and costumes popular in those days, used particularly by the people of Rajasthan, and in other parts of India as well. (Singh, 1991, 176-182)

From the Indus Civilisation till date, artists have striven to depict the wide range of Indian textiles in a variety of art forms.

An embroidered silk lehenga *from Gujarat. 19th century, National Museum, New Delhi.*

A satin silk lehenga *from Gujarat. 20th century, National Museum, New Delhi.*

white, among others) with resist double-dyed *ikat* technique, these *patola*s have either geometric or floral patterns all over. These saris have a special social significance. The Vora community of Muslims usually wear saris with geometric and floral patterns during weddings. Saris with plain, dark-coloured body, and borders depicting *nari-kunj* (women and birds) patterns are worn by Maharashtrian Brahmins. Jain and Hindu women prefer patterns all over: flowers, parrots, dancing figures and elephants, among others. Besides *zari* and silk woven saris, the tie-dyed patterned and *zari*-woven *gharchola* sari is special: it is woven with gold checks all over and has tie-dyed patterns within the checks. Among some ethnic groups in Gujarat, the bride wears a brilliant red *gharchola*. *Bandhej* saris have intricate patterns such as the *bavanbagh* (fifty-two gardens), the *ras-mandal* (associated with *dandiya*, the traditional dance of Gujarat), or the *amba dal* (mango branch) with peacocks, elephants and women dancing with their hands raised.

Besides the sari, the second most common traditional wear of Gujarati women is *ghagra*, *choli/kurti* and *odhani*. The *ghagra*, the long flared skirt, is similar to the one used by women in North India.

The highlights of the West Indian *ghagra* is its elaborate embellishment in bright colours—either an elaborate pattern woven on the fabric or intricate embroidery. Intricate patterns are made with *zari* and silk threads at the time of weaving the yardage, and the *ghagra* is embroidered with multicoloured silken thread, small mirrors, or sequins. Over the *ghagra*, women wear a *choli* or a *kurti* as an upper garment. The choli has multicoloured embroidery on the sleeves and in the front. *Choli*s and other garments with extensive mirrorwork are quite common, especially during folk dances like the *rasa*, *dandiya* and *garbha*, to name

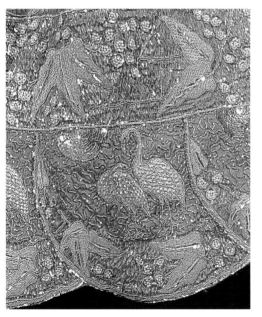

a few. The *kurti* is a sleeveless, jacket-like breast piece. It is longer than the other two garments and reaches the waist with buttons in front at the centre.

The *paithani* sari is the speciality of Maharashtra. Intricately woven with silk and *zari* thread, these saris are known for their soft, soothing colours and large-sized *kalka boteh*, lily-patterned *pallu* or end-piece on a golden background. Stylised flora-fauna usually figure in the borders.

The sari is worn with one of the

Top: *A blouse embroidered with gold thread, from Gujarat. 20th century, National Museum, New Delhi.*

Left: *The detail of a matching* lehenga.

Facing page:
The detail of a matching odhani.

A Mashru paijama from Gujarat. 19th century, National Museum, New Delhi.

of *choli*, and the difference between the *choli* used by Maharashtrian and Gujarati women lies in the raw material used for making them, and at times in the cuts.

The sari is worn over a petticoat (long skirt). In the days of yore, some women did wear a *paijama* under the sari.

Besides the production of drape or unstitched garments, a variety of yardage (*mashru, himru, bandhej*, printed, painted) is produced to make different types of stitched garments. *Mashru* is usually used for *paijama*s for both women and men, and as lining for men's upper garments. Muslim men have religious reservations about silk touching the body, so the weavers created *mashru* (literary 'permitted'), a combination of silk and cotton yarns. The *mashru* yardage is woven in such a manner that the cotton yarn touches the body and the silk yarn falls towards the outside. Bright-coloured *mashru* is usually created with geometric, zig-zag, or striped patterns.

Mashru is known for its glossy look, whereas *bandhani*, or tie-dyed fabric, is known for its brilliant dotted patterns. The most intricate and

following: *angiyaa, choli, kacoli,* or *kurti*, an upper garment used by the women of the Western region. The *choli* or *kacoli* is cut in a variety of ways: round or V-neck, short sleeved or sleeveless, open-back or back-fastening. These are usually embroidered with colourful threads and embellished with small mirrors and sequins. The *angiyaa* or *choli* is an open-back breast covering fastened with two pairs of tie-cords at the back. The Maharashtrian women use a similar type fine-quality *bandhej* fabric is from Saurashtra and Kutch (Gujarat): the plain fabric is tied following the pattern and dyed accordingly. Use of more than two colours while dyeing needs special care and skills. *Bandhej* is produced on plain cotton, muslin, and *gajji*, or satin silk. Sometimes *bandhej* is done on the golden check-patterned base *gajji*, popularly known as *gharchola*. Gujarati brides wear *gharchola odhani*s or saris. The blue-black tie-dyed *odhani*, with gold-embroidered borders, is used by Khatris for weddings along with the *abao* (loose shirt or gown) and the *salwar* (baggy trousers).

Printing and painting with mordant dye is also typical of the techniques used in Ahmedabad, Kutch, Jamnagar and Bhavnagar. The fine line work and the intricately designed geometric and floral motifs are made with brilliant and smooth colours. Such printed yardage is often used for making garments for men, women and children. The high level of skill involved in making wooden printing blocks, producing small and large pieces for domestic and foreign markets, and carrying through printing techniques efficiently, indicate the finely honed tradition of printing and dyeing on cotton cloth.

Apart from embroidery, *patola*, *bandhej* and *mashru*, Gujarat has a tradition of *zari* and silk brocade also. Brocade yardage with flora-fauna designs are created, from which costumes are made. The *tanchoi*, made from silk and *zari* yardage, is mainly popular among Parsis.

Apart from cotton and silk, woollen *dabla*s or *chaddar*s are also used by the people of this region because of their exposure to wide changes in day and night temperatures. *Dabla*s are used by men as a covering and by women as half-saris. These are woven with intricate geometric motifs. During the process of making the *dabla*s, first the women, and then the weavers spin the domestic sheep wool. Men, preferably, weave the shawl. These shawls are woven on a narrow-width loom in two pieces, later joined with multi-coloured thread by women.

A variety of silk saris, embroidered *ghagra*s, cotton and silk *kameeze*s, satin silk *abao*s, cotton *badiyan*s and *kurisi*s, and brocaded *angarkha*s, *jama*s and *dabla*s are the main traditional garments of Western and Central India. This region, besides being one of the best cotton-producing zones in India, is also reputed to have the oldest tradition of cotton printing in the country.

SOUTHERN INDIA

Karnataka, Andhra Pradesh, Tamil Nadu, Kerala and Pondicherry form the Southern region of India. Geographically, this region has mighty rivers like the Narmada, Tapti, Krishna, Kaveri and Godavari; and ranges like the Satpuras and the Vindhyas, which separate it from the northern plains of India. The block of land to the south of the Vindhyas extends up to the Arabian Sea in the west. In the east the Mahanadi River flows into the Bay of Bengal. The mainland, rich in vegetation, boasts of impressive mountain ranges, the Western and the Eastern Ghats, and a very beneficial river system. Boundaries of hills, rivers, forests and the vast water bodies largely insulated Southern India from foreign invasions, especially from the North. By the time these invasions began, people of Southern India had evolved a distinct culture of their own, which they protected well for centuries. Southern India established early trade contacts with the outside world. It was renowned for its fine cotton production centres and intricate patterns dyed in madder and indigo, which were in great demand in Saudi Arabia, Southeast Asia, the Far East, Java, Sumatra and the Malay Peninsula. The artisanal skills of this region were highly appreciated – colourful printed cottons, *zari* and silk-woven saris, and silk-dyed, *ikat*-woven fabric. From the 14th century onwards, some traders with trade links with Southern India developed their colonies at Calicut, Pondicherry and Madras. The indigenous people had close interaction with the foreign traders and produced work according to the demands of the market. Personally, however, they

Facing page:
The sari is an integral part of every Indian woman's wardrobe.
Photo courtesy: Rta Kapur Chishti

preferred their own traditional garments, mainly unstitched drape. Loose drape costumes were more appropriate for the people of this region climatically as well. Therefore, the textiles and costumes of this region were not too influenced by the outside world.

Traditionally the *dhoti*, *kurta*/shirt, *angavastram* and turban form the ordinary dress for men in Southern India. The *ghagra*, *choli/blouse* and *odhani* comprise the traditional dress for women. Women of this region prefer the

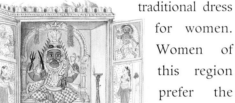

sari, so there exists a rich tradition of cotton, silk and *zari*-woven saris. There are various tribal people also, who wear bright and colourful costumes. Within the scope of this chapter, however, some of the traditional costumes worn by the men and women of Southern India will be discussed in detail.

Cotton-weave impressions on pottery found at T. Narasipur (Karnataka) belong to an early phase of the Southern Indian Iron Age (*c.* 1400-600 BC). Finds of terracotta spindle whorls and metal needles corroborate that the tradition of cotton weaving existed at the Chalcolithic sites of India. (Allchin, 1997, 428, 429) Terracotta, stone and bronze sculptures, and epigraphic inscriptions also provide important clues to the prevalent trends of textiles and costumes.

The epics give us many details of the culture of the people in the south, and also about the development of social and political life. They are useful in understanding the geography of Southern India and also its contacts with Ceylon, Malay and Indonesia.

The Sangam literature and the epics of South India, *Silappadikaram* and *Manimekalai* (1st century BC–3rd century AD), inform that cotton- and silk-weaving traditions existed during this period. The *Purana*s throw light on the history of the Satavahanas and the Rashtrakutas. Of the *Purana*s, the *Matsya* and *Vishnu Purana*s are the most informative on social history and prevalent traditions in costumes and textiles. Jaina, Buddhist and Prabhanda literature in Tamil reflect the socio-political and cultural life of the people in the far south during the early reigns of the Cholas, Cheras and Pandyas.

Foreign accounts—*Periplus of the Erythrean Sea* and *Geography* of Ptolemy—reveal the commercial and maritime activities of the South Indians. The Chinese traveller Hiuen Tsang visited India in the 7th century AD and stayed in the court of Emperor Harshavardhana. He travelled through Karnataka during the reign of the Chalukyan emperor Pulakesin II (r. *c.* AD 610-642), and visited the Tamil country. His travel accounts are replete with details on Southern India.

At the time of the Vijayanagara Empire, many European travellers (Portuguese, Dutch and Russian) and Arabs visited Southern India. Their accounts refer to the costumes used by the royalty and the common man. Inscriptions of Asoka, the Satavahanas, Gangas, Cholas, Hoysalas and the Vijayanagara Empire also reveal the social, political and cultural life of the people of those times.

The architectural ruins of Pattadakal, Aihole, Belur, Halebid and Hampi reveal the socio-political, economic and cultural conditions of the respective time-frames. The sculptures of these times depict the different types of costumes of deities and devotees as well.

Murals and miniature paintings of the Satvahana period (Ajanta, Cave no. 10, 2nd century BC), the Vakataka period (6th century AD), the Pallava period (7th century AD), the Pandya period (7th-9th

A bare-footed, wandering couple dressed in a Spartan manner, from Southern India. 19th century, Victoria and Albert Museum, London.

Sari: Poetic Elegance

~

Of all kinds of stitched and unstitched garments worn by the Indian woman, the sari is considered to be the most elegant. A typical sari is approximately 5.5 metres long and 1.3 metres wide, worn by folding, pleating and wrapping in such a way that it covers the entire body from head to toe. In Maharashtra and Karnataka, women wear saris that are nine yards long.

The term 'sari' originates from the Sanskrit words *shati* and *shatika*, which appears for the first time in the Panchatantra (I, 144, dating back to the 5th century AD).

Numerous literary, epigraphic, numismatic and sculptural references to the sari testify to the continuity of this garment, perhaps the oldest indigenous attire. Women in the Vedic period wore an *antariya* (lower garment), an *uttariya* (upper garment) and a *kayaband* (waistband). Gradually, from the Sunga and Kushan periods, we have descriptions of a garment that is like a sari.

From early references, it appears that initially the sari was the only garment worn by women. With time, however, a *choli* (upper garment) was added to this attire. A petticoat (long skirt) was further added to this ensemble, making it the three-piece attire that it is today.

As is clear in literary references and aesthetic representations of the past, the sari has been worn in many different styles. The most frequent wearing styles are the *kachcha* style; the *nivi* style;

Above and below: Details of a baluchari *sari from West Bengal; Middle: A woman from Southern India; 19th century, Victoria and Albert Museum, London.*
Facing page: *A* gharchola *sari from Gujarat.*
Photo courtesy: Rta Kapur Chishti.

Women in Chennai dressed up in rich and colourful Kanjeevaram silk saris on a ceremonial occasion. The elderly lady has worn her sari differently from the other ladies in the photograph. The young girls are wearing the lehenga-choli.
Despite the popularity of Western outfits in India, on special occasions people prefer to wear traditional costumes. Photo courtesy: V. Muthuraman.

and a combination of the *kachcha* and *ghagra* styles. These different wearing styles lend variation to the outfit. Even today, women in Maharashtra wear the sari differently from those in Bengal, Gujarat, or North India. Interestingly, women of Madhya Pradesh and Chattisgarh wear the sari in more than ten different styles.

A cotton sari with simple design is generally used as everyday wear, while bright-coloured silk saris are normally worn on special occasions like festivals or weddings.

At present, the handloom industry of India is busy in the production of saris. Weavers create magic by producing saris from various kinds of material such as muslin, cotton and silk. These saris are woven with designs ranging from human beings to animal figurines, birds and floral motifs. They are either embellished on the loom itself (*jamdani*, *baluchari*, *zari*, or *ikat*) or woven plain and later embellished through block printing, *bandhani*, or embroidery.

The world over, people are bound to concede that the sari remains one of the most elegant attires for women.

In India, a sari could well be 'a woman's best friend'. Photo courtesy: Rta Kapur Chishti

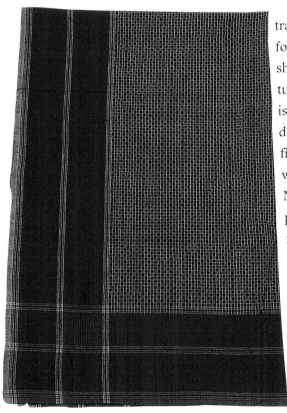

A cotton telia rumal, also worn as a loincloth by men of the fishermen's community, from Andhra Pradesh. 19th century, National Museum, New Delhi.

Facing page:
A woman welcoming a Brahmin, Southern India. 19th century, Victoria and Albert Museum, London.

centuries AD), the Chola period (9th-13th centuries AD) and the Nayaka period (17th-18th centuries AD) provide important information on the costumes of the respective periods. These paintings are replete with beautifully illustrated turbans, tunics and *dhoti*s worn by men. Saris, *choli*s and *kamarband*s were worn by women. Necklaces, earrings, crowns and bangles were an important part of the accessories used by the people of this region.

The most common traditional costume for men is *dhoti*, shirt, *angavastram* and turban/scarf. The *dhoti* is worn in two distinctive styles: the first is the standard wearing style of Northern India—the pleats are tucked in front in such a manner that the whole bunch, when tucked in, leaves no space between the buttocks and the innermost pleat of the bunch. In the second wearing style, the *dhoti* is wrapped around the loins without any gathers or pleats either at the back or in the front. The *dhoti* then hangs as a straight skirt without any gathers, much like a *lungi*. Usually, men wear a white cotton *dhoti* with a narrow colourful border. Sometimes these *dhoti*s are colourful or with check. Some paintings of the Vijayanagara and Nayaka periods depict men wearing *dhoti*s with checks or floral patterns.

The *angavastram* or body-cloth or scarf is commonly used by men in Southern India. Usually it is wrapped around the waist, at times twice and at others more than twice, as is portrayed in the stone sculptures at the Brihadisvara Temple. Men cover their heads with a headgear that is freshly wrapped, rather than a pre-formed turban. The size and volume of the headgear varies with the provenance as well as the nature of the caste group. The 17th-century paintings of the Nayaka period (housed in the Madras Museum) depict Yudhishtira's coronation, with men wearing *dhoti*s, *angavastram*s and turbans on the occasion. A courtesan is depicted wearing the *jama*, the *paijama* and the Maratha-style turban, all quite colourful. (Sivaramamurti, 1968, 136, Fig: 88)

Apart from the usual costumes worn

by common men, there is a fishermen community in Andhra Pradesh that wears a special kind of loincloth, popularly known as *telia rumal*. These cotton *telia rumals* are woven with *ikat* technique in maroon, white and black. These *rumals* can be used in a variety of ways—as a *lungi*, a turban, and a scarf to be thrown over the shoulders. The main weaving centre of the *telia rumal* is Chirala. Golconda used to produce elaborate hangings and square *rumals* with designs drawn from miniatures. These *rumals* also feature various people who once lived in this region—Chinese, Arabs, and the indigenous people identifiable by their costumes. Long *jamas*, tunics, *paijamas*, Chinese turbans and sashes have been portrayed in these *rumals*.

Women of Southern India usually wear two kinds of attire—the sari, blouse and petticoat, and the *ghagra*, *choli* and *odhani*. The sari is wrapped around the waist, the pleats tucked in front, and the front then covered by the end-piece. (Sivaramamurti, 1968, 118, Fig. 72) The tight-fitting bodice is used as an upper garment, completing the ensemble. The bodice is knotted in front, just below the breasts, with two flaps. In a number of paintings, women have been portrayed

wearing saris that are quite colourful, with a variety of patterns.

The tradition of sari weaving in Southern India yields a rich variety of saris. The silk *ikat* saris from Pochampalli, the Kanchipuram silk and *zari*-brocaded saris of Tamil Nadu, and the Karalkudi (white

cotton with *zari*) of Kerala constitute some of the best-known sari traditions of the South. The silk *pallu* and border with a cotton body, of the *Gadwals* and *Wanapartis* of Andhra Pradesh, are famous for their quality work. Rich, gold-brocaded saris are made for weddings or for offering to temples. Apart from silk brocades, a range of cotton saris from Tamil Nadu have brilliant checks, and contrasting border and *pallu*. The cotton-woven *jamdani* and the intricate weave of *Venkatagiris* are equally renowned for their workmanship. The royal family of Tanjore patronised special cotton and *zari*-brocaded saris from the Kadalikaruppar area. These saris combine finely woven cotton with motifs worked in *jamdani* weave in gold thread.

Material (cotton, silk, *zari*), patterning and designing vary according to region and caste. The type and volume of saris vary both with provenance and the ethnic group residing in that area.

Women wear the sari in different styles. Some ethnic groups first wrap the sari around the waist, then take it between the legs, and tuck it at the back. The end-piece is used for covering the upper part of the body.

Women of Southern India also wear the *ghagra*, *choli* and *odhani*, usually made of either *zari* and silk brocade or cotton.

The *thali* (*mangalsutra* or wedding necklace), the *nathu* and *ballakku* (nose-ring and nose ornaments that hang over the upper lip), girdles of 32 strings of pearls, the *oddiyuanam* (belt), the *vanki* (amulet), the *rakkodi* (hair-pin) and the *matlal* (eartops) are some important jewellery worn by women. Most of the South Indian jewellery is made of gold with precious stones like diamonds and rubies.

Southern India had a rich tradition of Indian classical dance, apart from regional folk dances. The folk dancers wear their

गरुरुरुडहशुभांगी जलराभापात्रचक्रधरिभय
इरिरैवननीलाणी सिनपक्षरूट्टर्यीअसेदिख १२

colourful ethnic costumes. The three classical dance forms, among the six main classical dance forms of India, Bharat Natyam, Kuchipudi and Kathakali are from Tamil Nadu, Andhra Pradesh and Kerala, respectively.

Bharat Natyam (Tamil Nadu) is the oldest classical dance. It derives its name from Bharat Muni, who wrote the *Natya Shastra*, a treatise on dance, music, stage-setting, poetry, costumes and make-up. In this dance form the dancer is usually a woman. The dancer's costume consists of a brocade sari. Neatly arranged brocade pleats hang in the middle from the waist to the knees, with a *choli* covering the upper part of the body, jewellery, and the *veni* (floral garland) adorning the dancer's hair.

Kuchipudi, a dance-drama of Andhra Pradesh, can be traced back to the times of the Satavahana kings of the 2nd century BC. The costume consists of a brocade sari and *choli* for the female dancer, while men wear silk *dhoti*s and lots of jewellery such as necklaces, earrings, *bajuband*s, bangles, anklets and rings.

Kathakali represents India's ancient tradition of enacted and sung dramas. The elaborate costume, the mask make-up and the gorgeous crowns are reminiscent of its folk traditions. The costume consists of pleated, billowing white skirts, long-sleeved tunics with red, ornamented breast-plates, and yards of cloth garlands ending in rosettes.

Colourful silk brocade saris, *dhoti*s, and cotton and silk woven saris are worn by women of this region. The *dhoti*, *kurta* and *patka* are commonly worn by the men. Foreign influence, however, is obvious, especially on the costumes of the people

A telia rumal from Andhra Pradesh. 19th century, National Museum, New Delhi.

Facing page:
Ragini Kakubha in a ghagra, choli *and* odhani, *from Andhra Pradesh. c.1775, Bharat Kala Bhawan, Benaras.*

of Pondicherry, which was ruled by the French in the 18th–19th centuries. Trousers, shirts, hats, skirts and tunics are some of the common dresses used by men and women in this region. The tribal

Various ethnic groups who came to this region from different parts of the world and settled here, have enriched the indigenous world of Indian textiles. Being adaptable, Indians accepted their tradition

people also wear multicoloured costumes and textiles. Special dresses, materials and colours are associated with festive and religious occasions.

and taught them indigenous customs. The world of Indian costumes and textiles, therefore, straddles a vast and varied cultural and sociological landscape.

GLOSSARY

aanchal	Pallu or end-piece, the most integral part of a sari.
achkan	A man's long-sleeved, coat-like garment, worn close to the body, reaching down to the knees or lower, and buttoned down the centre in front.
angarkha	Literally 'which protects or covers the limbs.' An outer garment with long sleeves for men, open at the chest and tied in front with an inner flap or *parda*, full-skirted, and of varying lengths.
angavastra	Cloth for the body.
angavastram	Sanskrit word meaning *patka*, *kayaband* (Hindi), or *sash*, used by men as a waistband over the upper garment.
antarvasaka	Upper garment.
ashawalli	Silk and *zari*-brocaded sari woven in twill technique in Ahmedabad, Gujarat.

bagalbandi	Type of short tunic or jacket, fastened under armpits.
balabar	*Angarkha*-like outer garment worn by men.
baluchari	Silk brocaded sari of Baluchar in Murshidabad, West Bengal.
bandhej	Process of patterning cloth by tie-dyeing, in which the design is reserved on the undyed cloth by tying small spots very tightly with thread to protect them from the dye. Most popular in Rajasthan and Gujarat.
bandiyan	Short, round-necked, half-sleeved upper garment worn by men.
batik	Dye-resist technique mainly popular in Southeast Asian countries. Wax is used for resist.
buteh	Literally *buteh*, *buti*, or *buta*, it means 'plant'. The motif is sometimes reduced to a floral pattern designed within the form of the

Note: Terms already explained earlier in the book are not mentioned in this section.

	plant. Usually a big-sized floral pattern.
butidar	Small-sized, floral-patterned field.
chaddar	Shawl used by men and women; also *chandes* or *chaddar*.
chakdar jama	*Jama* (see below) with *chak*s (slits).
chapkan	*Angarkha*-type outer garment with some European features. Open at centre front, with a U-shaped neck, the waist has a curved cut and the skirt has panel on the right which crosses over the left and is fastened at the left side with a pair of tie-cords.
chikan	One of the finest varieties of embroidery done with white cotton thread on white cotton cloth.
choga	Loose, sleeved, coat-like garment of Turkish origin worn over an inner garment like the *angarkha*. This front-open, full-length attire is considered to be an appropriate dress for ceremonial occasions. Variously known as *chogha*, *chuba*, or *juba*.
choli	A short, bodice-like breast garment popular among women in India, from early times worn in many styles: with back covering; with tie-cords; or as extended cloth-pieces with shaped breast pieces. Other terms for *choli* in classic Sanskrit literature are *angiya*, *cholaka*, *chola*, *cholika*, *kanchuka* and *kancholika*.
churidar paijama	From *churi*, or bangle-like gathers or wrinkles. Tight-fitting, trouser-like lower garment with such gathers towards the lower portion.
dhakkai mulmul	Muslin made in Dacca in present-day Bangladesh.
dhoti	Long, unstitched fabric used as a lower garment by men almost all across India. The most common wearing style is to wrap it around the waist, gather the rest in front, and take the gathered bit between the legs and tuck behind.
dupalli topi	Small, close-fitting cap with two identical pieces.
dupatta	Veil/scarf also known as *odhani*, *dupatta*, *chunni*, or *chunari*, draped loosely over the upper part of the body by women.
farshi paijama	Wide-legged, trouser-type lower garment that trails on the ground, sometimes completely covering the feet; worn often with a *kurta* or an *angarkha*.
gajji	Satin fabric.
ghagra	Skirt with lots of gathers worn by women. The simple *ghagra* has only one vertical seam, which transforms the cloth or *ghagra pata* into a tube, fastened with drawer-strings. Flared *ghagra*s are made of several gored triangular pieces stitched together.
himru	Silk and cotton brocaded fabric of Aurangabad, Maharashtra.
huqqa	Vessel with four or five parts used for smoking tobacco. The base is filled with water, with two pipes attached to it; one pipe holds the *chilam*, the container for the

tobacco, and the second pipe is used for smoking through the *muhnal* or mouthpiece. Around the late 18th-early 19th centuries, the *huqqa* was the most popular way of smoking tobacco among men and women across the country.

ikat — From the Indonesian word *mengikat*, meaning 'to tie' or 'to bind'. A dye-resist process in which designs are reserved in warp or weft yarns by tying off small bundles of yarn with palm-leaf strips or similar material to prevent penetration of dye.

jama — Full-sleeved, knee-length, or longer outer wear for men snugly fitted at the chest with high waist seam and flared skirt. It was tied under the right or the left armpit with tie-cords.

jamdani — Pattern of extra weft, without floats. Earlier, Dacca was famous for producing fine *jamdani*. Later, Tanda (near Lucknow, Uttar Pradesh) and Varanasi (Uttar Pradesh) also became famous for producing *jamdani* fabric, from which garments are made.

jilucha — Kind of gown.

kachcha — Hindi term used for shorts-like lower garment. *Kachcha*-style *dhoti* refers to the *dhoti* worn short.

kalamkari — Cloth hanging of South India made through printing and painting done by the kalam (pen). It illustrates scenes from epic.

kalka — *Ambi* or mango-shaped pattern popularly known as paisley.

kameez — Full-sleeved, long shirt usually worn by men, and at times by women as well.

kanchuka — Bodice or upper stitched garment worn with the sari by women. Also known as *kanchuki*.

karkhana — State-governed workshop and storehouses established by rulers during the medieval period for the production of things used by them.

kasaba — Kind of cap worn by married princesses; also known as *qasaba*.

kulah — Skullcap.

kurta — Literally 'tunic, waistcoat, jacket, shirt.' Worn by men and women, the *kurta* is a slightly loose-fitting, knee-length, and longer outer garment, often with a round neck and side slits.

lungi — Long, straight cloth worn by men in a range of styles.

mashru — Fabric woven from silk warp and cotton weft yarns. Literally 'in accordance with the *sharia* or the Islamic Holy Law.'

mirzai — Type of jacket, often equated with a 'quilted coat'. Usually worn sleeveless over a shirt as an outer garment; sometimes worn next to the skin. Plain or sometimes woven or printed with religious mantras, the *mirzai* is worn only on religious occasions.

muga — Variety of silk.

nakshi kantha — *Kantha* is a hand-embroidered quilted covering of Bengal, usually with geometric and floral motifs. Figurative, patterned kantha is known as *nakshi kantha*.

namavali chaddar	Shawl with the name of a deity either woven or printed.
nawab	An official rank during the Mughal rule, bestowed according to one's political stature and military power.
nima	Type of tunic; modified version of a *kurta*, usually made of fine material. Also known as *nimatana* or *nimcha*.
paijama	Trouser-like garment, worn by men and women alike. Literally 'leg-clothing'. Also known as *churidar paijama*, *sidha paijama*, or *farshi paijama*, depending on shape and cut. The *paijama* varies in girth, length, fit and material.
paithani	Silk and *zari*-brocaded sari woven in tapestry weaving technique, one of the oldest weaving techniques of India, at Paithan, Maharashtra.
pashmina	Fabric made from *pashm* wool.
patka	Girdle or *kamarband*, with very decorative patterns woven or embroidered on its panels, worn usually over a *jama* by men.
patola	Double *ikat* of Patan, Gujarat, made with silk thread. Both warp and weft yarns are tied and dyed in a calculative manner, so that once it is woven on loom the entire pattern appears on it.
peshwaz	Long, gown-like dress, consisting essentially of a *choli* worn rather high and a skirt that has a front opening.
petticoat	Stitched long skirt worn under a sari.
phiran/pirahan	Loose, cloak-like shirt reaching down to the feet, used by both men and women in Kashmir.
phulkari	Literally 'flowered work'; used for embroidery with floss silk thread upon coarse cotton cloth, done by the women of Punjab on head scarves and other garments.
rasa	Literally 'mood'.
sadri	Sleeveless jacket worn over a shirt or *kurta*, by men and women alike. Derived possibly from *sudrat*: the upper part of the human chest.
salwar/shalwar	*Paijama*-like lower garment, baggy and wide at the top, and loosely fitted around the legs and ankles. Worn mostly by women, but also by men, especially in the northwest.
sanghati	Double waist-cloth
sari	Long unstitched fabric wrapped around the waist, its end-piece falling either in front or at the back, with variations in regional wearing styles.
sherwani	Knee-length, coat-like garment, worn by men, with front opening and button fastenings. Similar to the *achkan* and especially popular at the Hyderabad court and in Aligarh.
sidha palla	Sari wearing style in which the end-piece is taken over the right shoulder and covers the front.
taat	Cotton fabric.
tanchoi	Derived from *tran choi*, that is, the three Choi brothers who learnt this art of weaving

in China and introduced the technique in Surat. Done with silk yarn.

tangail	Silk brocaded sari of Bengal.
telia rumal	Tie-dyed scarf woven in Andhra.
topi	Cap.
tus	Finest variety of wool obtained from the Himalayan goat.
ulta palla	Sari wearing style in which the end-piece is taken under the right armpit,

over the left shoulder, and draped at the back.

upanah	Sanskrit term for 'shoe'.
usnisa	Turban or headgear usually worn by men. Also known as *sapha*, *pag*, or *pagadhi*.
uttarasanga	Mantle.
zardozi	Type of embroidery in which metallic (gold or silver) threads are sewn on satin or velvet.
zari	'Gold' in Persian; *zari*: thread made of *zar*.

BIBLIOGRAPHY

Abu'l Fazl Allami, *Ain-i-Akbari*, (tr) H. Blochmann 2nd edition, Delhi, 1965

Afif S.S., *Tarikh-I-Firuzsaahi*, (ed) Hussain Vilayat Maulvi, Calcutta, 1890

Agrawala, D.P., *The Archaeology of India*, London, 1982

Agrawal, V.S., *Harshacharita: Ak Sanskitk Adhayan*, Patna, 1964

Aijazuddin, F.S., *Sikh Portraits by European Artists*, Delhi, 1979

Ali, Yusuf A., *A Monograph on Silk Fabrics Produced in the N.W. Provences and Oudh*, Allahabad, 1959

Alkazi, R., *Ancient Indian Costumes*, Delhi, 1983

Allchin, F.R., 'Textile Impressions from the South Indian Iron Age,' in *A Sourcebook of Indian Archaeology*, Vol. II, 1997

Allchin, B. & R. Allchin, *The Rise of Civilization in India and Pakistan*, Cambridge, 1983

Alam, I., 'Textile Tools as Depicted in Ajanta and Mughal Painting,' in *History of Science and Technology in India*, (ed) A. Singer, Vol. III, Delhi, 1990

Ansari, M.A., *Social Life of the Mughal Emperors*, Allahabad, 1974

Archer, W, G., *Indian Paintings from the Punjab Hills*, London, 1973

Asthana, S., 'Taxila Jewellery,' in *Masterpieces from the National Museum Collection*, (ed) S.P. Gupta, Delhi, 1985

Atharvaveda, Trivedi S., Allahabad, 1912

Babur, Zahirud-din-Muhammad, *The Babur-Nama*, (tr) Annette. S. Beveridge, 2 Vols., London, 1912-1922

Badaoni, P.B.H., *Handbook of Economic Products of the Punjab*, Lahore, 1872

Bahmania, K.R., 'Adorning the Self,' in *Alamkara* exhibition catalogue, Singapore, 1994

Bamzai, P.N.K., *History of Kashmir*, Delhi, 1973

Banerjee, J.N., *The Development of Hindu Iconography*, Calcutta, 1956

Barve, B.R., *Complete Textile Encyclopedia*, Bombay, 1967

Bence-Jones. M., *Palaces of Raj*, London, 1973

Bernier, F., *Travels in the Mogul Empire* (Indian edition), New Delhi, 1972

Bhatnagar. P., *Elementary Textile*, Chandigarh, 2002

Bhattacharya, S.K., in 'The Indus Civilization,' in *Masterpieces from the National Museum Collection*, (ed) S.P. Gupta, New Delhi, 1985

Bhushan, Jamila B., *The Costumes and Textiles of India*, Bombay, 1958

Buhler. A. & Marie. L. Buhler, *Indian Tie-dyed Fabrics*, Ahmedabad, 1980

Chandra, M., *Costumes, Textiles, Cosmetics and Coiffure in Ancient and Mediaeval India*, Delhi, 1973

Daljeet, *Mughal and Deccani Paintings from the Collection of the National Museum*, Delhi, 1999

Dames, M. L., *The Book of Duarte Barbosa*, Vol. I, London, 1918

Dar, S.N., *The Costumes of India and Pakistan*, Bombay, 1969

Desai, V.N., *Life at Court: Art for India's Rulers, 16th-19th centuries*, Festival of India, exhibition catalogue, U.S.A, 1985-86

Dhamija, J., 'Embroidery of Gujarat: Living Traditions,' in *Decorative Arts of India*, (ed) M.L. Nigam, Hyderabad, 1987

Dwivedi, S., *The Maharajas and the Princely States of India*, Delhi, 1999

Foster, W. (ed), *Early Travels in India*, London, 1921

Guy, J., *Woven Cargoes: Indian Textiles in the East*, London, 1998

Geijer, A., *A History of Textile Art*, London, 1979

Goswamy, B.N., *Indian Costumes in the Collection of the Calico Museum of Textiles*, Ahmedabad, 1993

Ghosh, A., *Ajanta Murals*, Delhi, 1967

Ghurye, B.N., *Indian Costumes*, Bombay, 1951

Jain. J. & A. Aggarwala, *National Handicrafts and Handlooms Museum*, Ahmedabad, 1989

Jahangir, Nurud-din Muhammad, *Tuzuk-i-Jahangiri*, (tr) A. Rogers and H. Beveridge (Indian edition), New Delhi, 1968

Kenoyer, J.M., *Ancient Cities of the Indus Valley Civilization*, Pakistan, 1998

Kahlenberg, M.H., 'A Study of the Development and Use of the Mughal Patka with Reference to the L.A. County Museum of Art Collection,' in *Aspects of Indian Art*, (ed) P. Pal, Los Angles, 1972

Kumar, Ritu, *Costumes and Textiles of Royal India*, London, 1999

Lal, B.B., *The Saraswati Flows On: The Continuity of Indian Culture*, Delhi, 2002

Lal, B.B., *India 1947-1997: New Light on the Indus Civilization*, Delhi, 1998

Mackey, E., 'Household objects, tools and implements,' in *Mohenjodaro and the Indus Civilization*, (ed) J. Marshall 3 Vols., London, 1931.

Mahavagga, (ed) Hermann Oldenderg, Vol. I, Bombay, 1879.

Majumdar, N.G., 'Exploration in Bengal,' in Annual Report of the Archaeological Survey of India (ASI), 1934-35

Majumdar, R.C., *The Vedic Age*, Bombay, 5th edition, 1988.

Maxwell, T.S., 'Devotion,' in *'In the Image of Man,'*

Festival of India, U.K., Exhibition catalogue, London, 1982

Marshall, J., *Taxila*, 3 Vols., Cambridge, 1951

Pal, P., 'Indian Terracotta Sculpture,' *Marg*, Mumbai, 2002

Pathak, A., *'Prithvi ki garbha me chhupi: pratham bunkaro ki kahani'* (in Hindi), *Sanskrti*, New Delhi, 2000

Possehl, G.L., *Indus Age—The Beginnings*, Delhi, 1999

Rau, W., 'Weaving in Vedic India,' in *Woven Fabric*, (eds) J. Dhamija & J. Jain, Ahmedabad, 1984

Randhawa, M.S., *Kangra Paintings of the Bhagvata Purana*, New Delhi, 1973

Rig-Veda, (ed) Shri Pad Damodar Satvlakar, Padri, 4th edition, 1981

Roe, T., *The Embassy of Sir Thomas Roe to India, 1615-19*, (ed.) Sir William Foster, New Delhi. Revised edition, Delhi, 1990

Roy, N., *Art of Manipur*, Delhi, 1979

Sahay, S.N., 'Ancient Textile Industry,' *Journal of Bihar Research Society*, 1973

Saraswat, K.S., 'Archaeobotanical Remains in Ancient Cultural and Socio-Economical Dynamics of the Indian Subcontinent,' in *The Paleobotanist*, 40, 2002-2003: 514-45

Sarasvati, S.S.P., *The Critical and Cultural Studies of Satapatha Brahamanam*, Delhi, 1988

Satapatha-Brahmana, Savanacharna, T., Part II, Bombay, 1940

Sen, G., *Paintings from the Akbar Nama*, Singapore, 1984

Sharma, R.C., *Buddhist Art—Mathura School*, Delhi, 1995

Shanti, S., *5000 Years of Art and Craft in India and Pakistan*, Bombay, 1968

Singh, C., *'Atharvi-unnisvishatime Rajasthan ki veshbhusha,'* *Shoda Patrika*, year 25, no. 3-4, Jaipur, 1974

Singh, C., *Textiles and Costumes from the Sawai Man Singh Museum, Jaipur*, 1979

Singh, C., 'Two medieval compositions on Indian textiles,' in *Pathways to Literature, Art and Archaeology*, Vol. I, (eds) Singh, C and Vashishtha, Neelima, Jaipur, 1991

Singh, K., *Textiles in Ancient India*, Varanasi, 1994

Sivaramamurti, C., *Amaravati Sculptures in the Madras Government Museum*, Madras, 1977

Sivaramamurti, C., *South Indian Painting*, Delhi, 1968

Strong, S., 'The Age of the Mughals,' in *Arts of India: 1550-1900*, (eds), John. Guy and Deborah Swallow, London, 1990

Taittireya Samhita, Shri Pad Damodar, Satvlakar, Padri, 2nd edition, 1957

Verma, M., *Ancient Indian Costumes and Ornaments*, Varanasi, 1989

Watson, F., *The Textile Manufactures and the Costumes of the People of India*, Varanasi, 1982

Welch. S.C. & A.S. Schimmel, *The Emperors' Album: Images of Mughal India*, New York, 1987

Yazdani G., *Ajanta*, The colour and monochrome reproductions of the Ajanta Frescoes based on photography, London, 1930

ACKNOWLEDGEMENTS

My gratitude for the support of my mentors for *Indian Costumes*: Ms. Krishna Lal, former keeper, National Museum, Delhi; Dr. Daljeet, Dr. N. Akhtar, Dr. S.V. Tripathi and Dr. R. Sharma, curators at the National Museum, Delhi; Rahul Jain, textile technologist; Dr. Chandramani Singh, director, Jawahar Kala Kendra, Jaipur, Rajasthan; and Dr. S.D. Sharotri, former professor, Meerut University. My indebtedness to well-wishers: Dr. N. Krishna, associate professor, National Museum Institute of Art, Conservation and Museology, Delhi; Dr. R. Sharma, curator, National Bala Bhawan, Delhi; Dr. Y. Agrawal, deputy keeper, Bharat Kala Bhawan, Benaras; and Ms. M. Krishna, freelance editor.

Special thanks to Dr. A.K.V.S. Reddy, director general, and Dr. U. Das, director, National Museum, Delhi, for giving permission to publish part of the invaluable collection of the National Museum, Delhi. Sincere thanks to Dr. A. Pandey, Government Museum, Mathura, and Dr. Deborah Swallow, curator, Victoria and Albert Museum, London, for allowing me to use photographs from their collections. A word of thanks to Smt. P. Pararsher, senior librarian and information officer, and to Ms. R.M. Bagra, B. Chobe, Ms. Anita and the staff of the National Museum library for their help during the making of *Indian Costumes*; to Shri J.C. Arora, photo officer, and T. Singh, photographer, for photographing the objects at the National Museum, Delhi. Special thanks also to the respective museum authorities for granting me permission to publish photographs from their collections, and to Rta Kapur Chishti and V. Muthuraman for allowing me to use photographs from their personal collections.

I thank Roli Books for giving me the opportunity to write *Indian Costumes*.

My most sincere thanks to my soulmate S.K. Pathak, my mother Urmila Dwivedi, and my children Anvita, Abhishek, Devansh and other family members, who provided unconditional support while I wrote *Indian Costumes*.

PHOTO CREDITS

All photographs/illustrations from the National Museum, New Delhi, except those listed below:

Bharat Kala Bhawan, Benaras: 12, 132, 134 (left)

British Library, Oriental and India Office Collections: 34, 56

Chishti, Rta Kapur: 116, 121, 124-125; Government Museum, Mathura: 20, 21

Karachi Museum, Karachi: 13; Muthuraman, V.: 122-123, 130, 135

The Royal Collection © 2006, Her Majesty Queen Elizabeth II: 41

Victoria and Albert Museum, London: 7, 19, 33, 48, 49, 52-53, 55, 58, 59, 61, 70, 118, 119, 120 (middle), 127

(Copying work at National Museum, New Delhi, done by Dheeraj Paul)